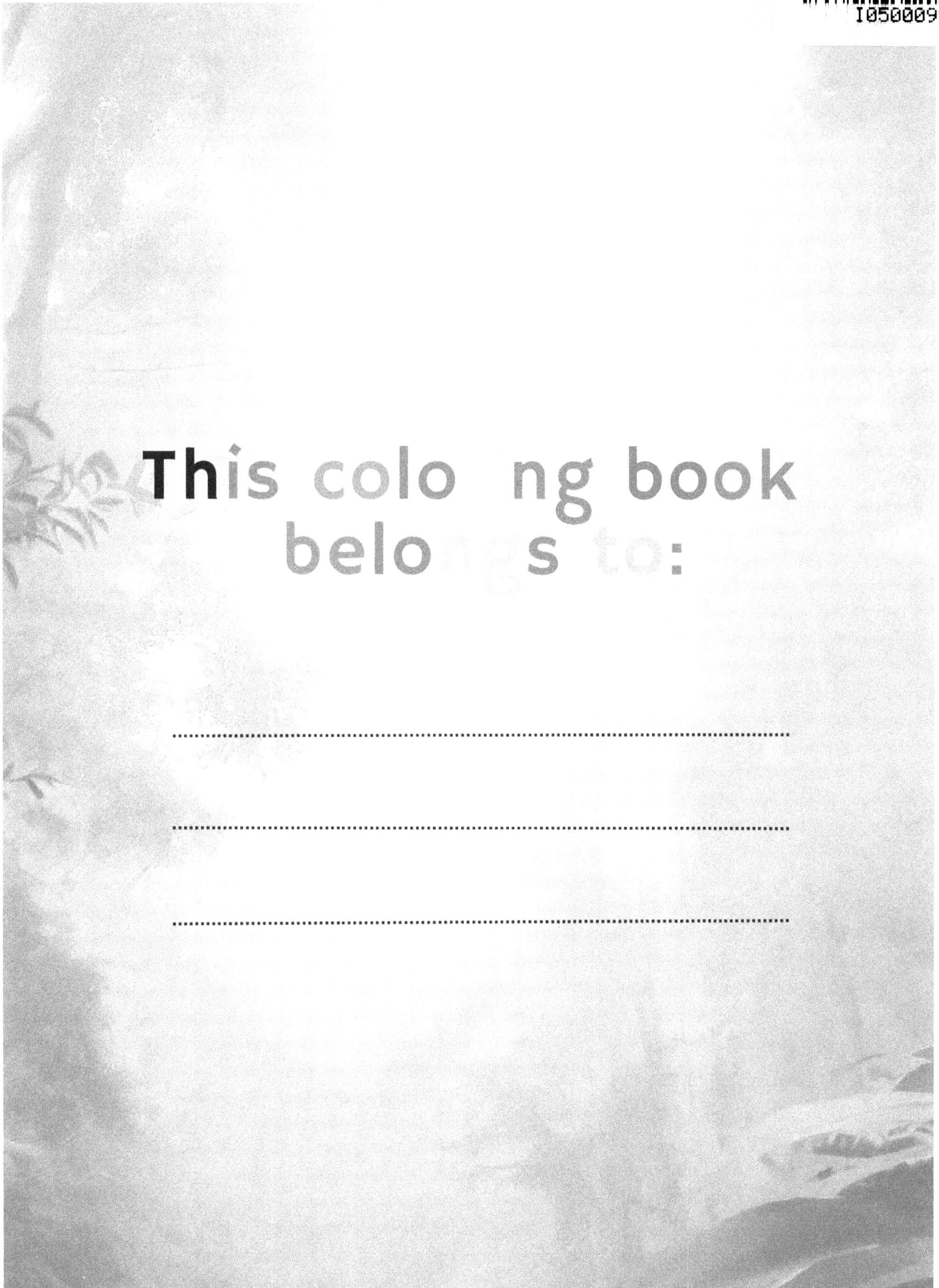

This coloring book belongs to:

....

....

....

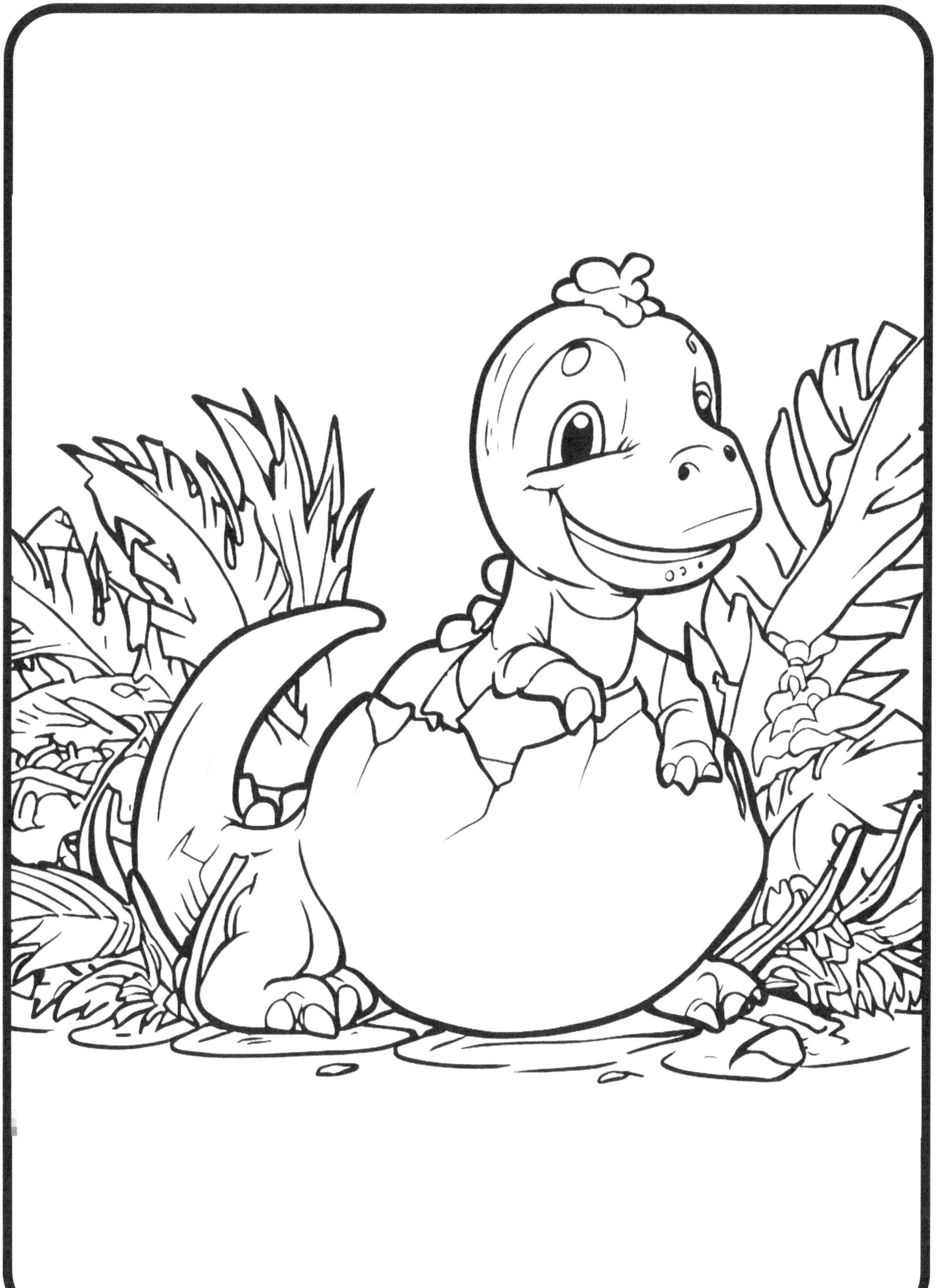

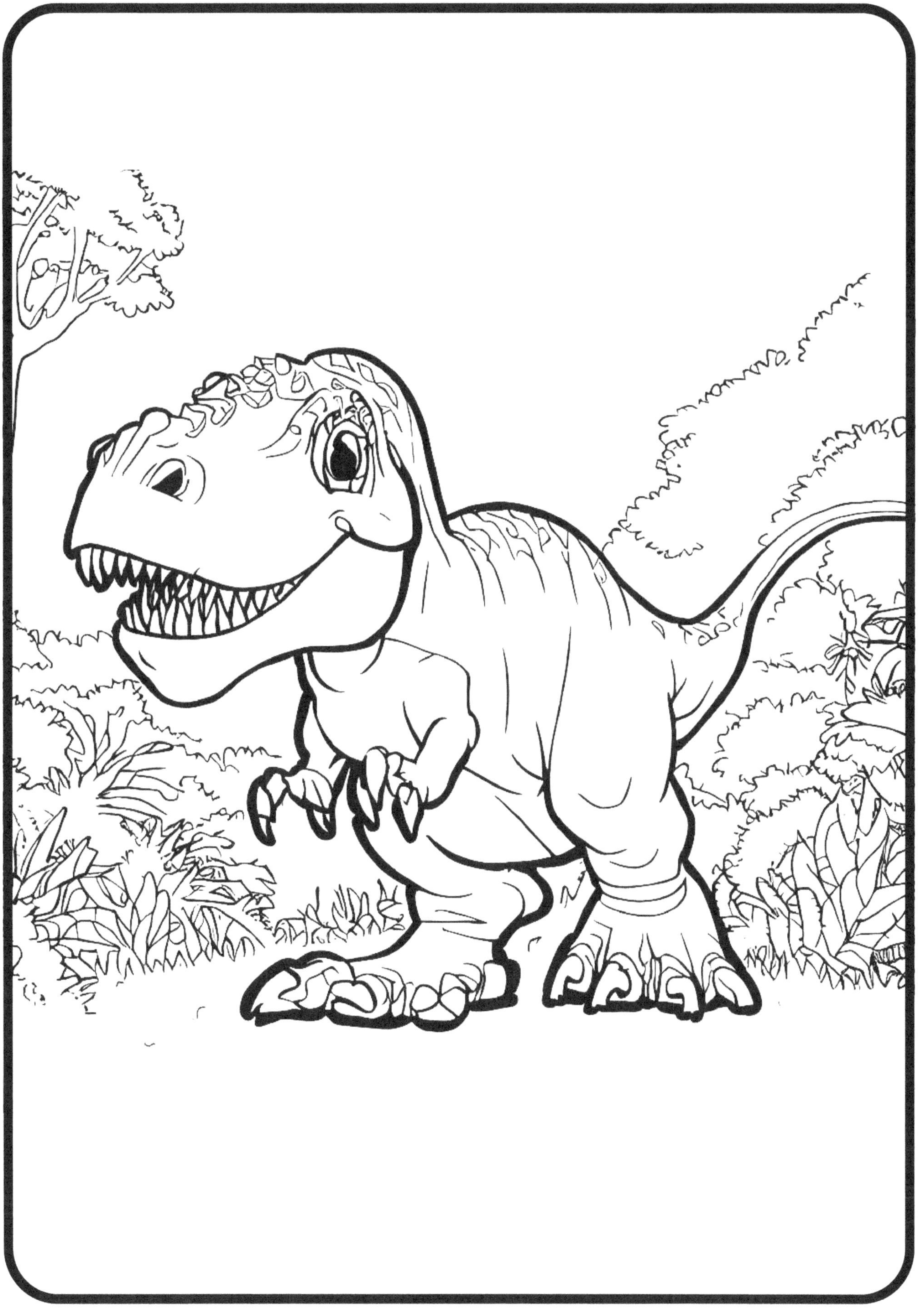

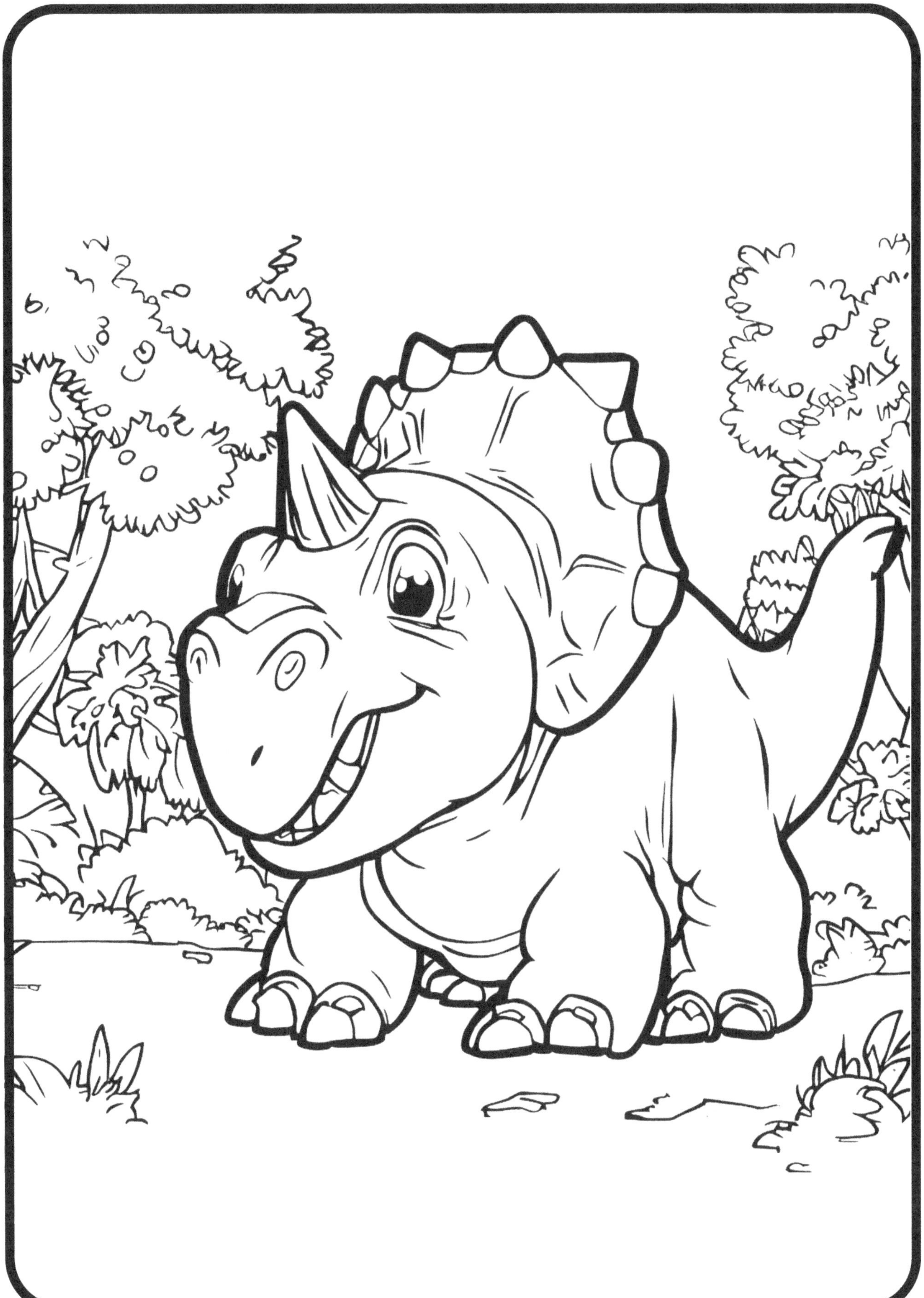

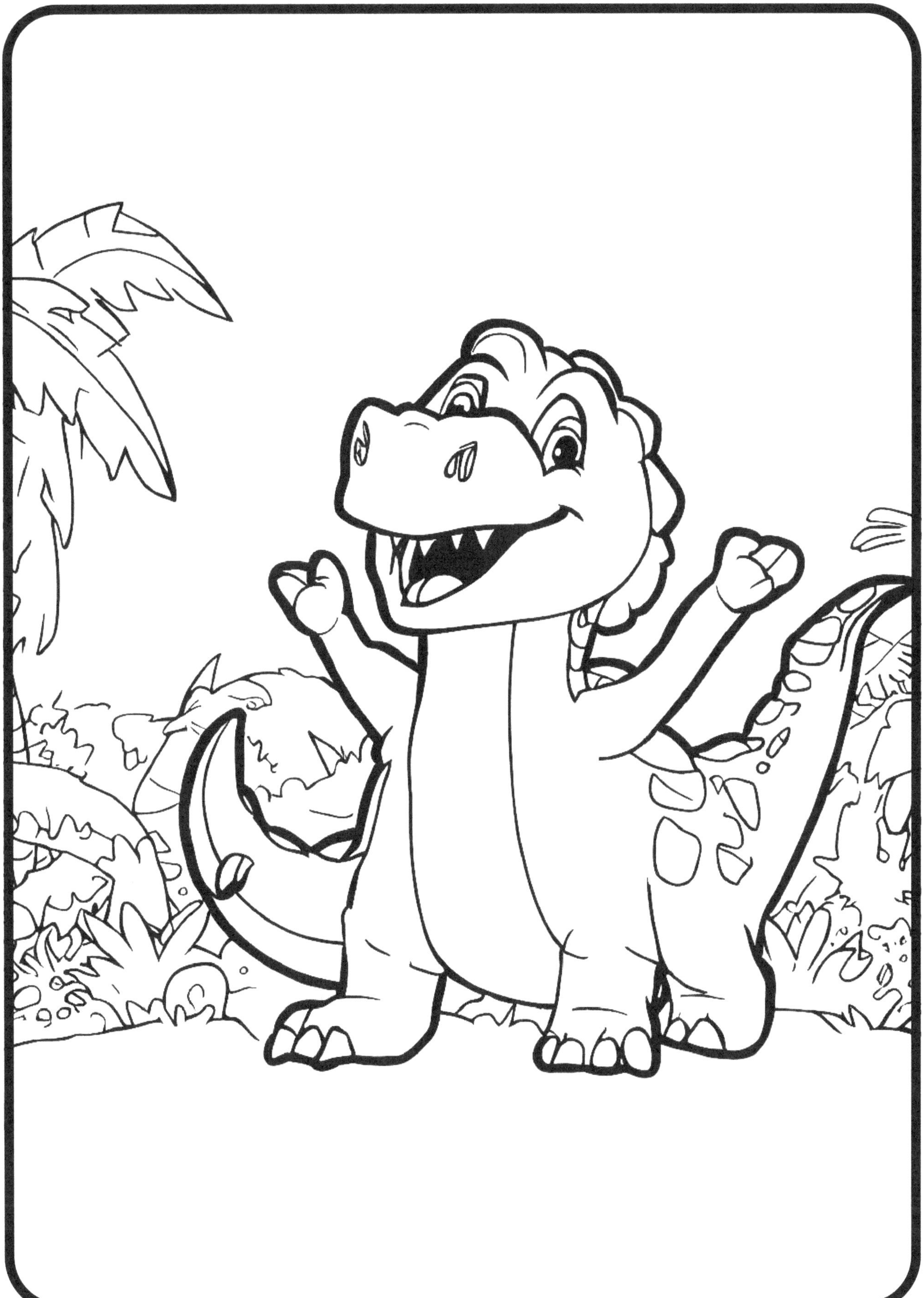

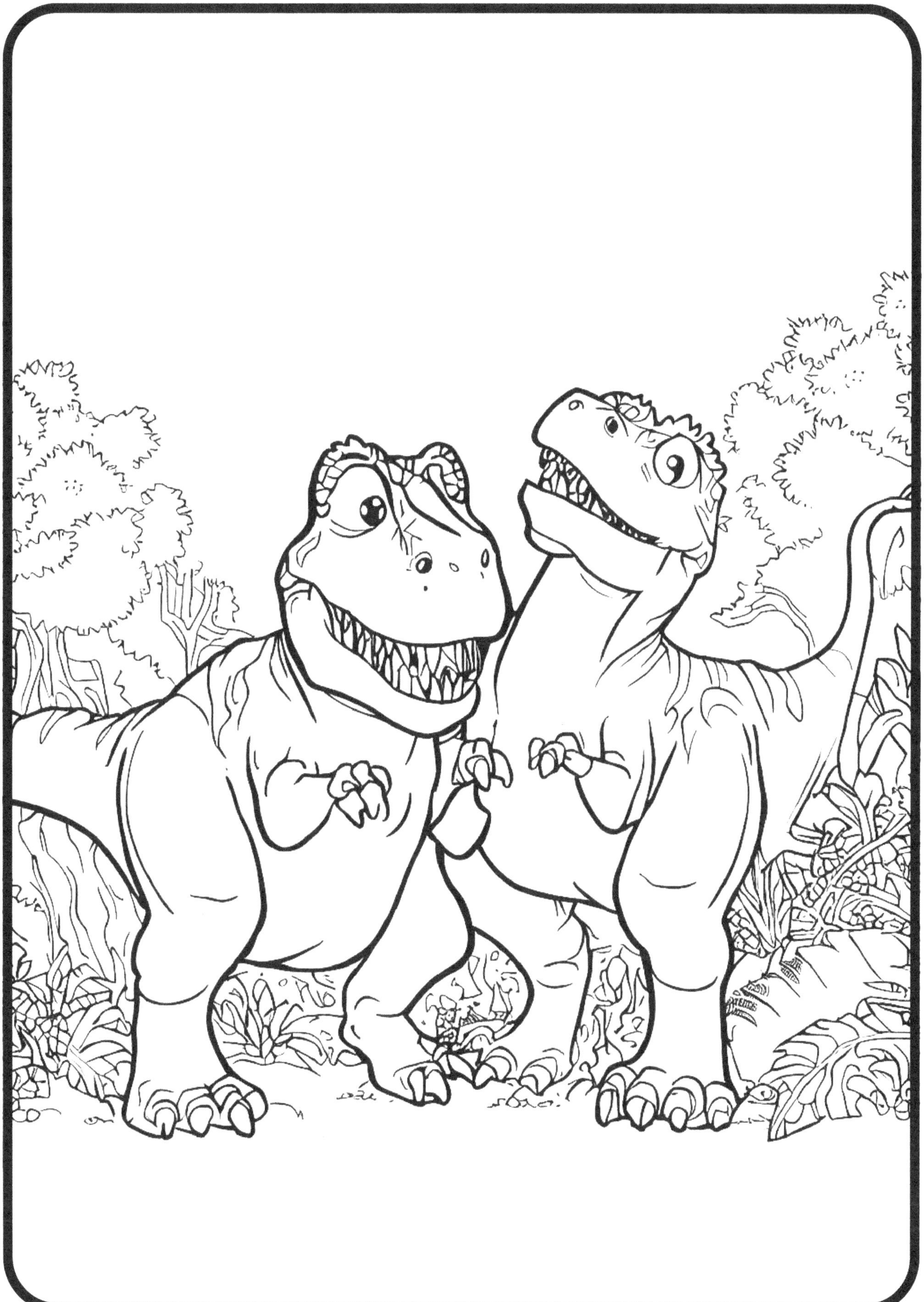

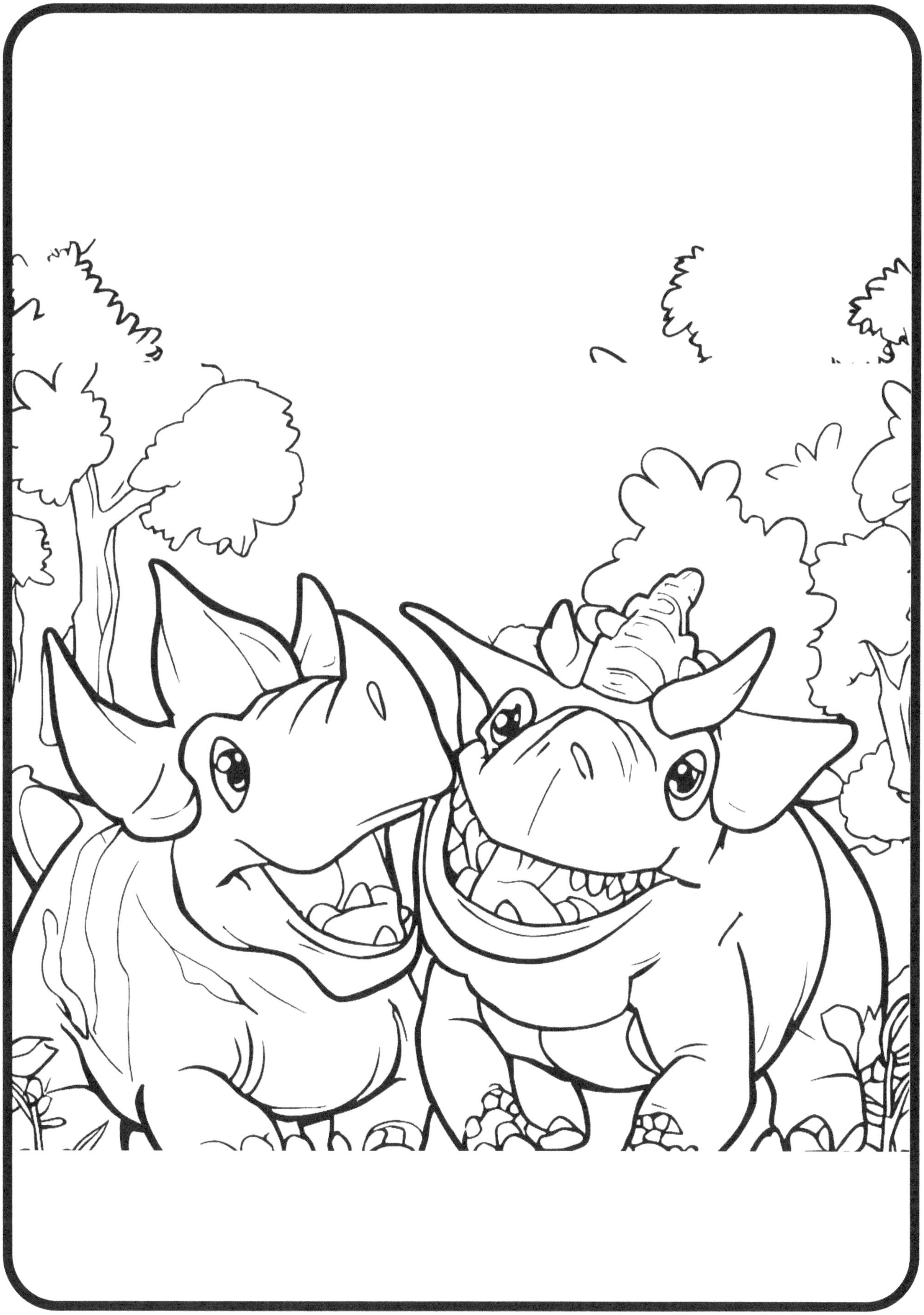

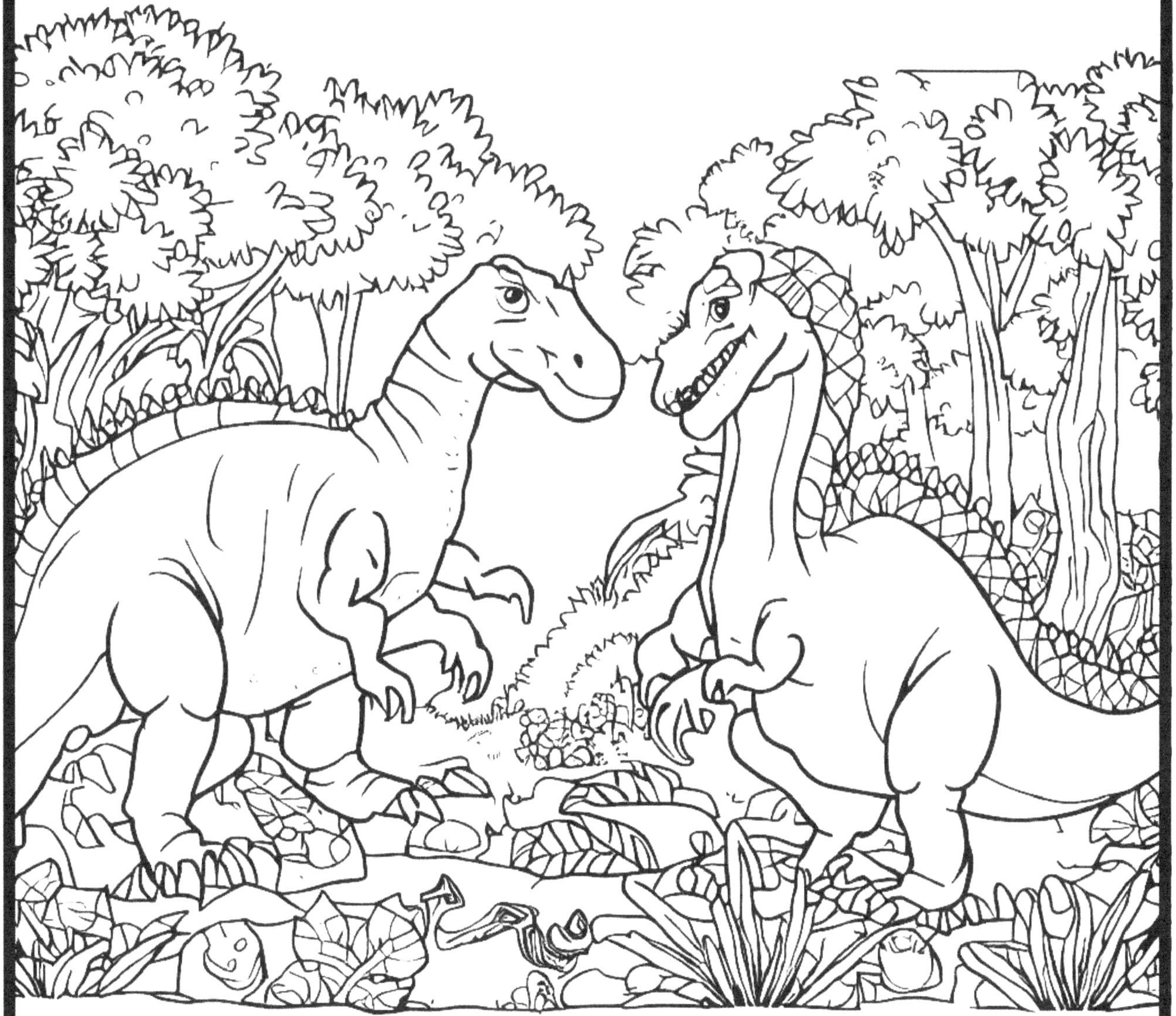

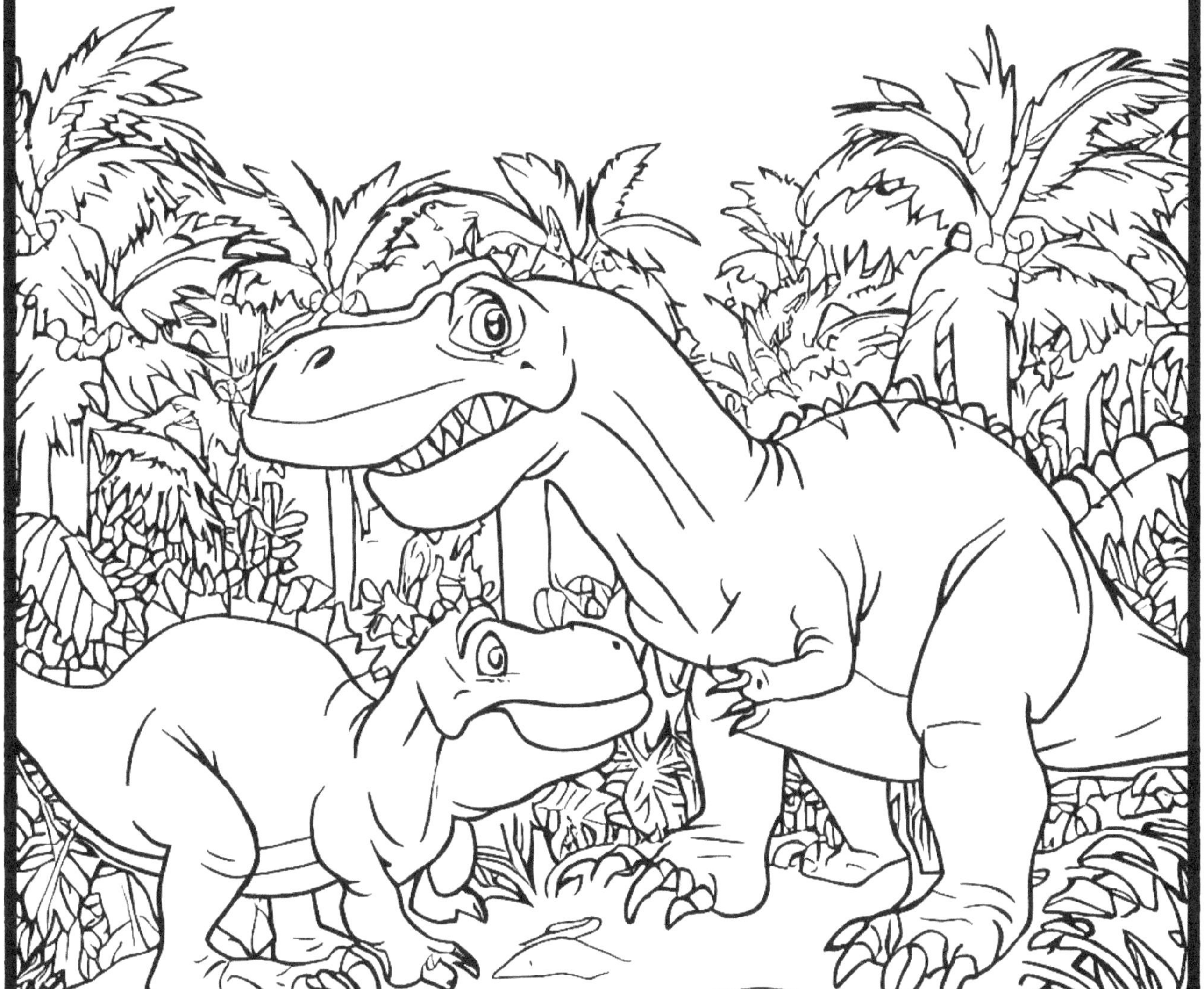

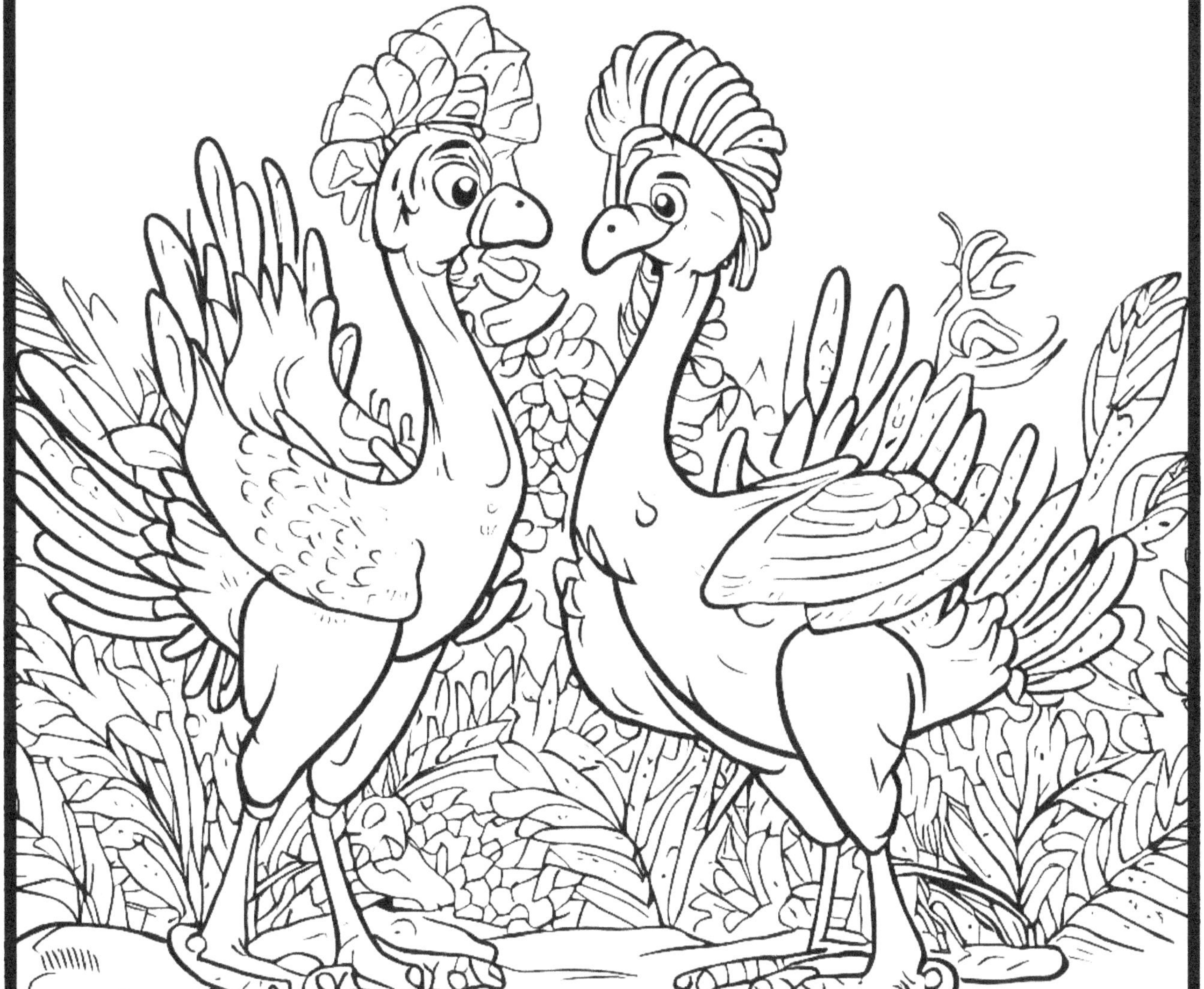

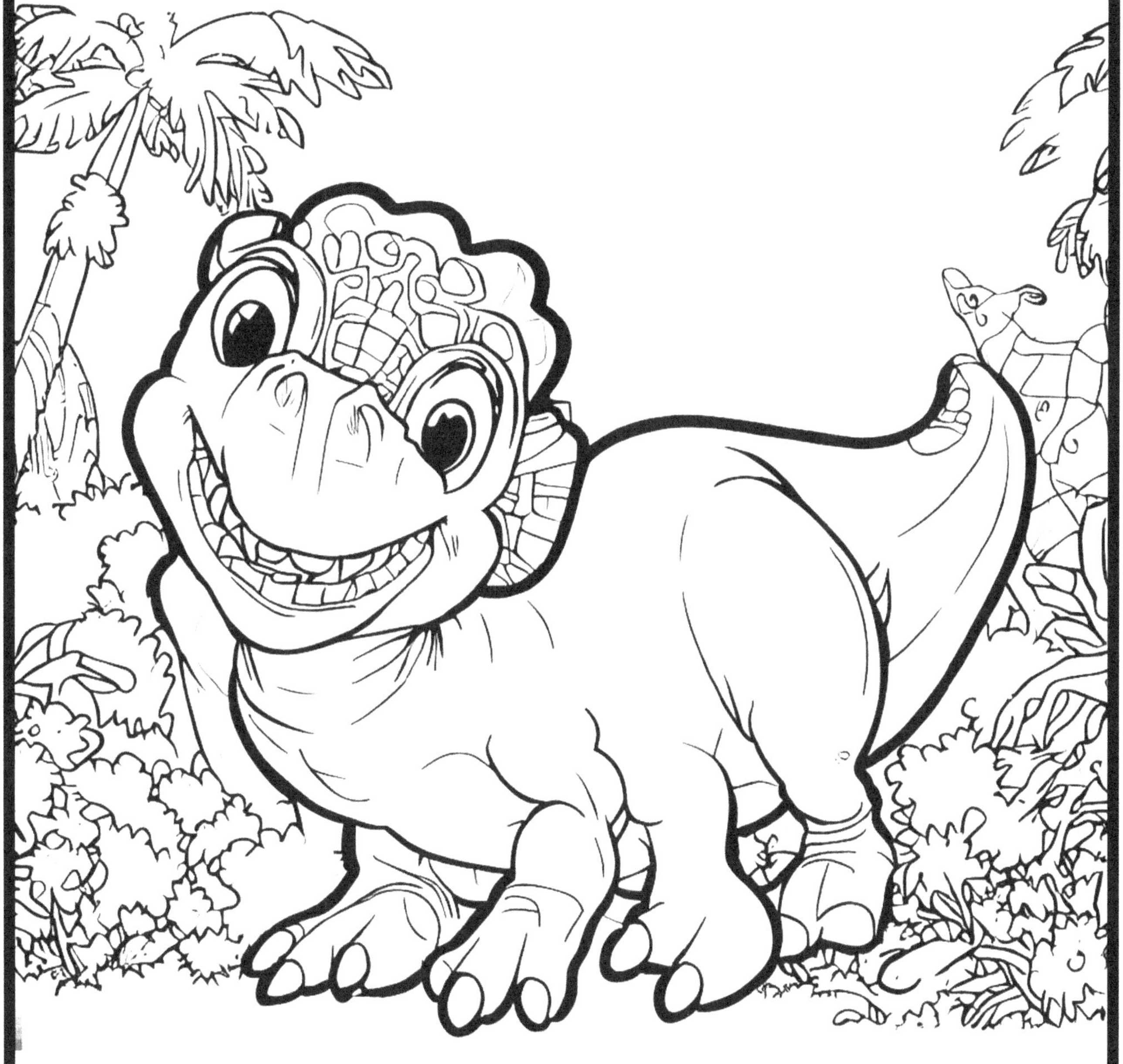

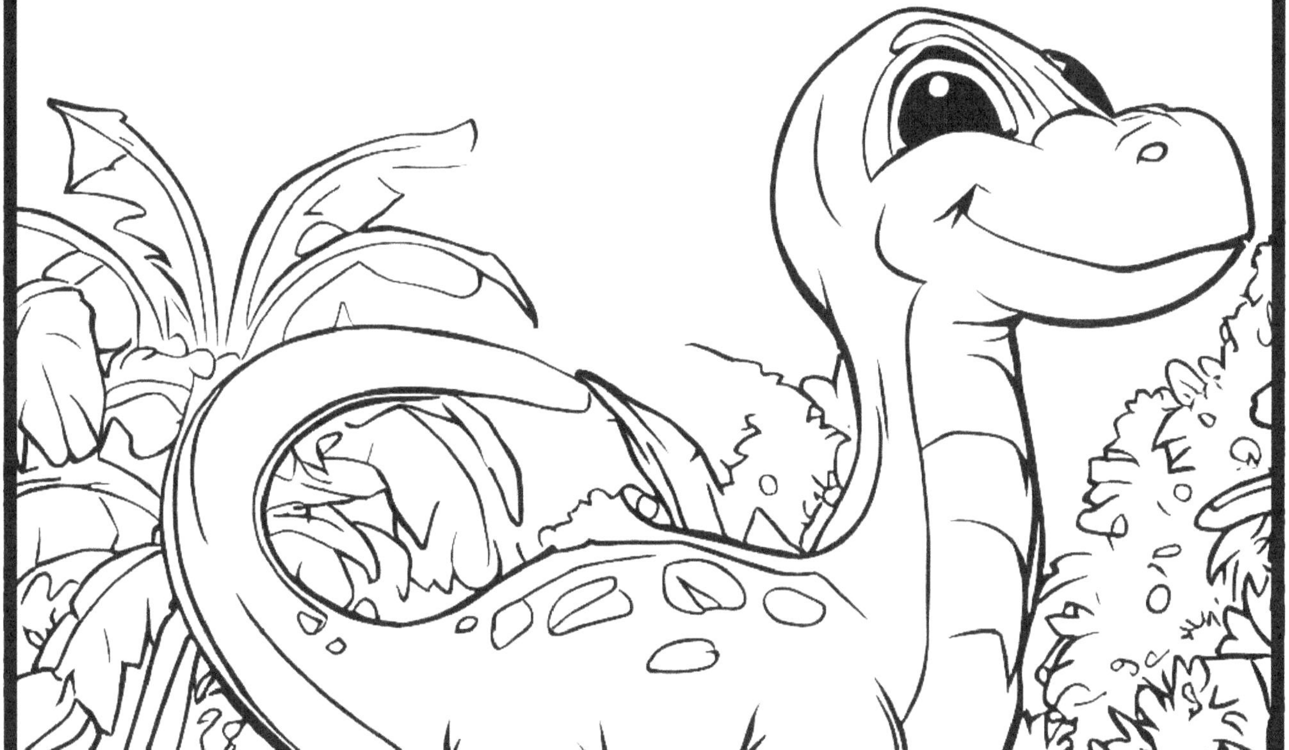

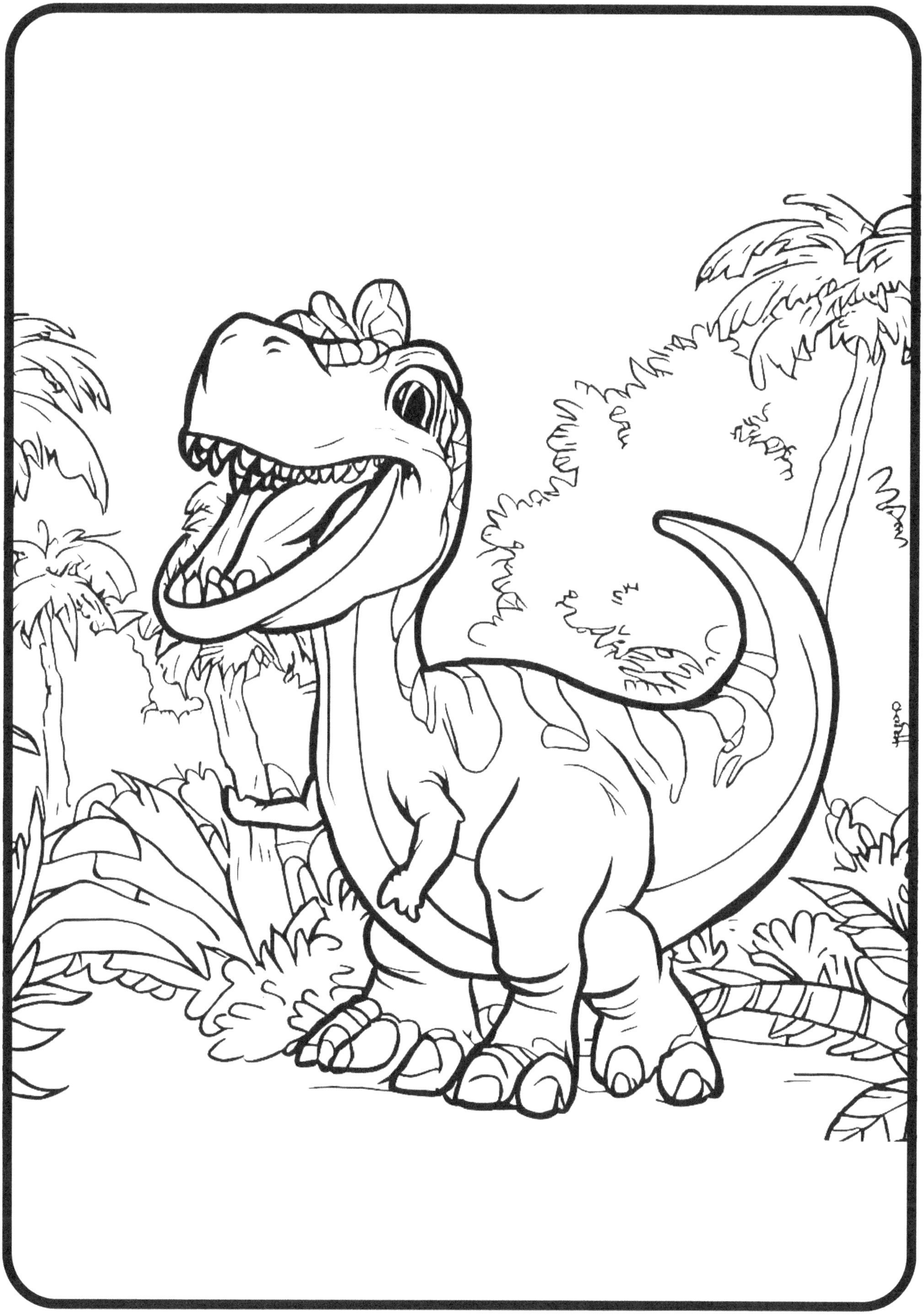

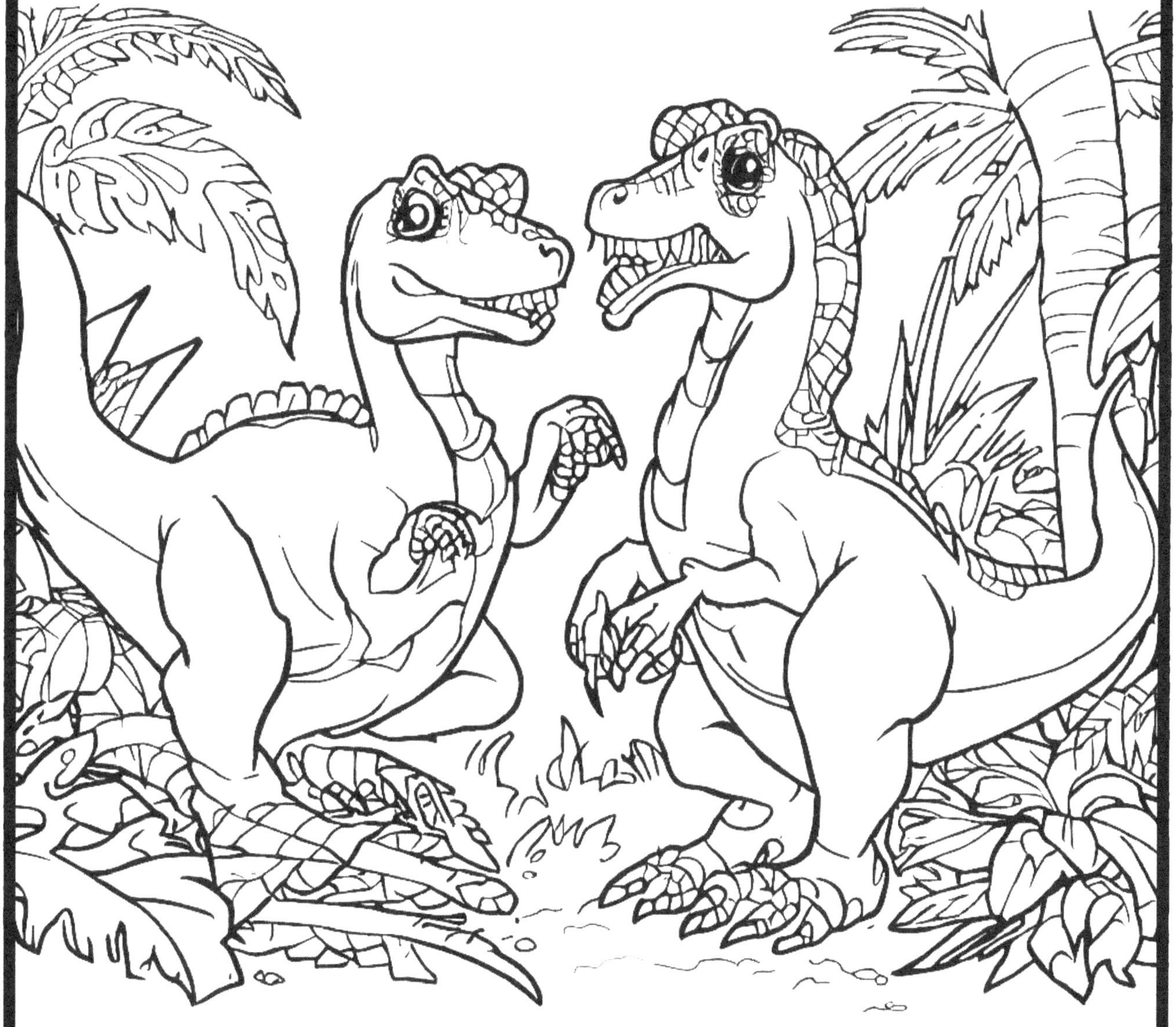

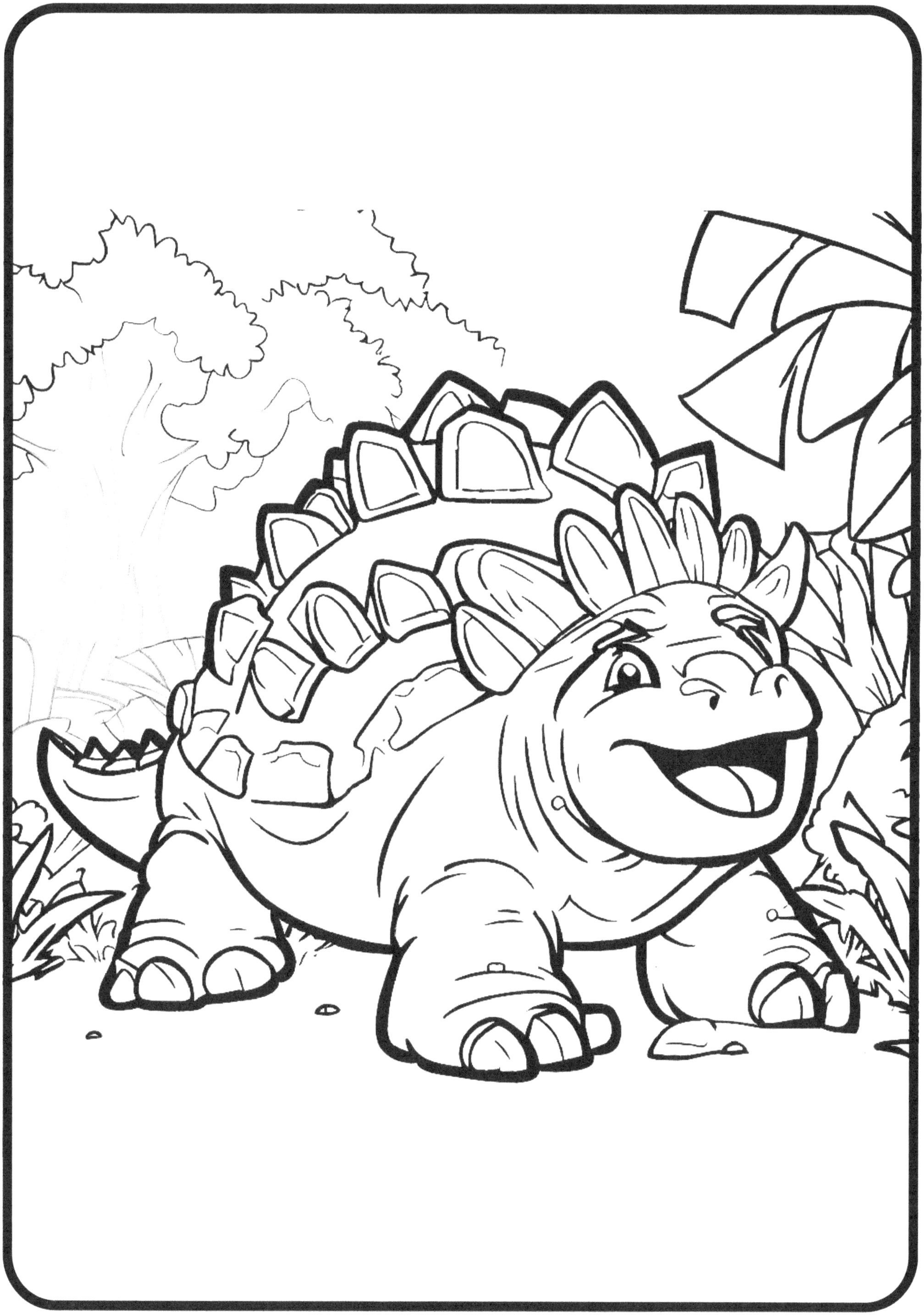

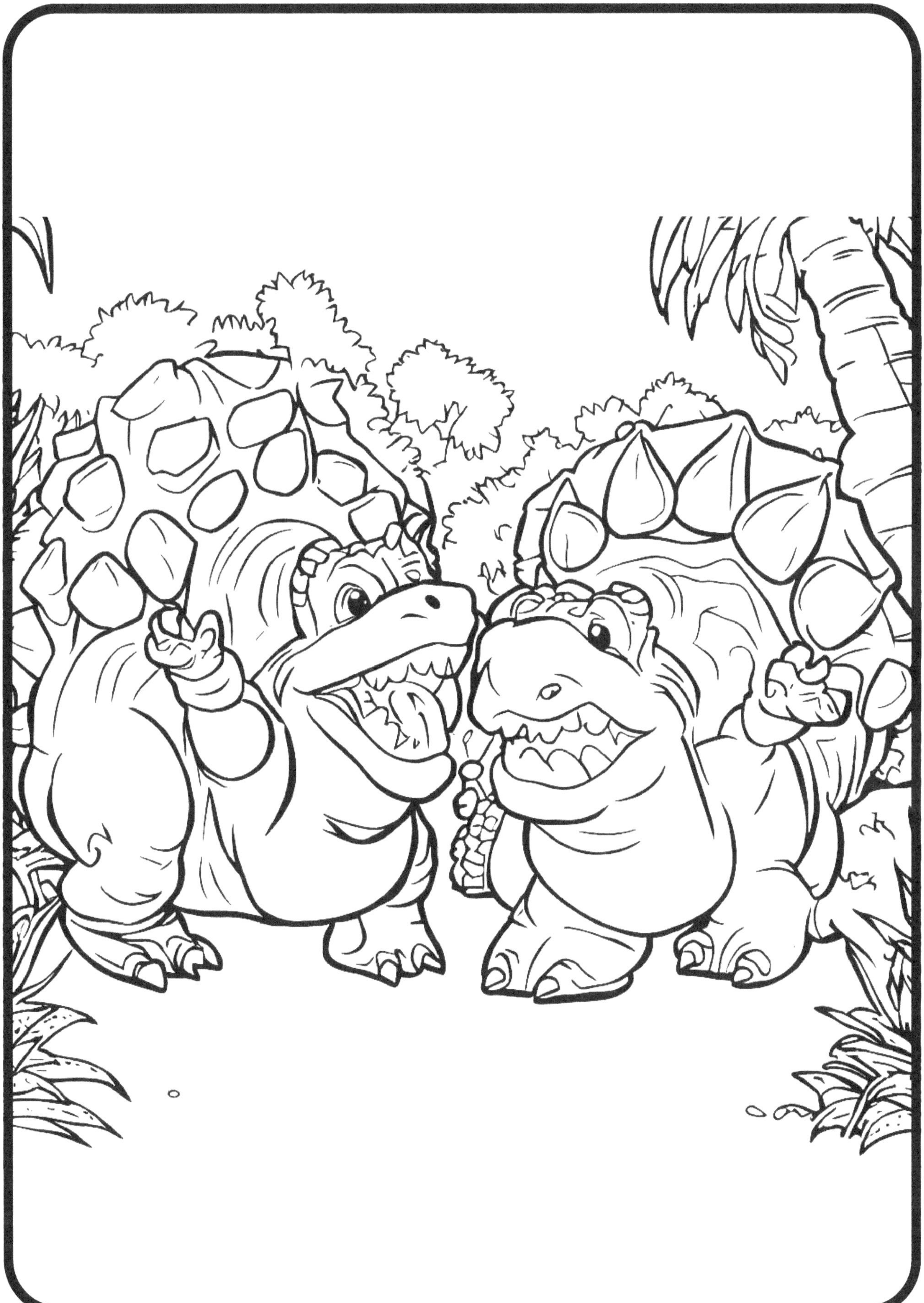

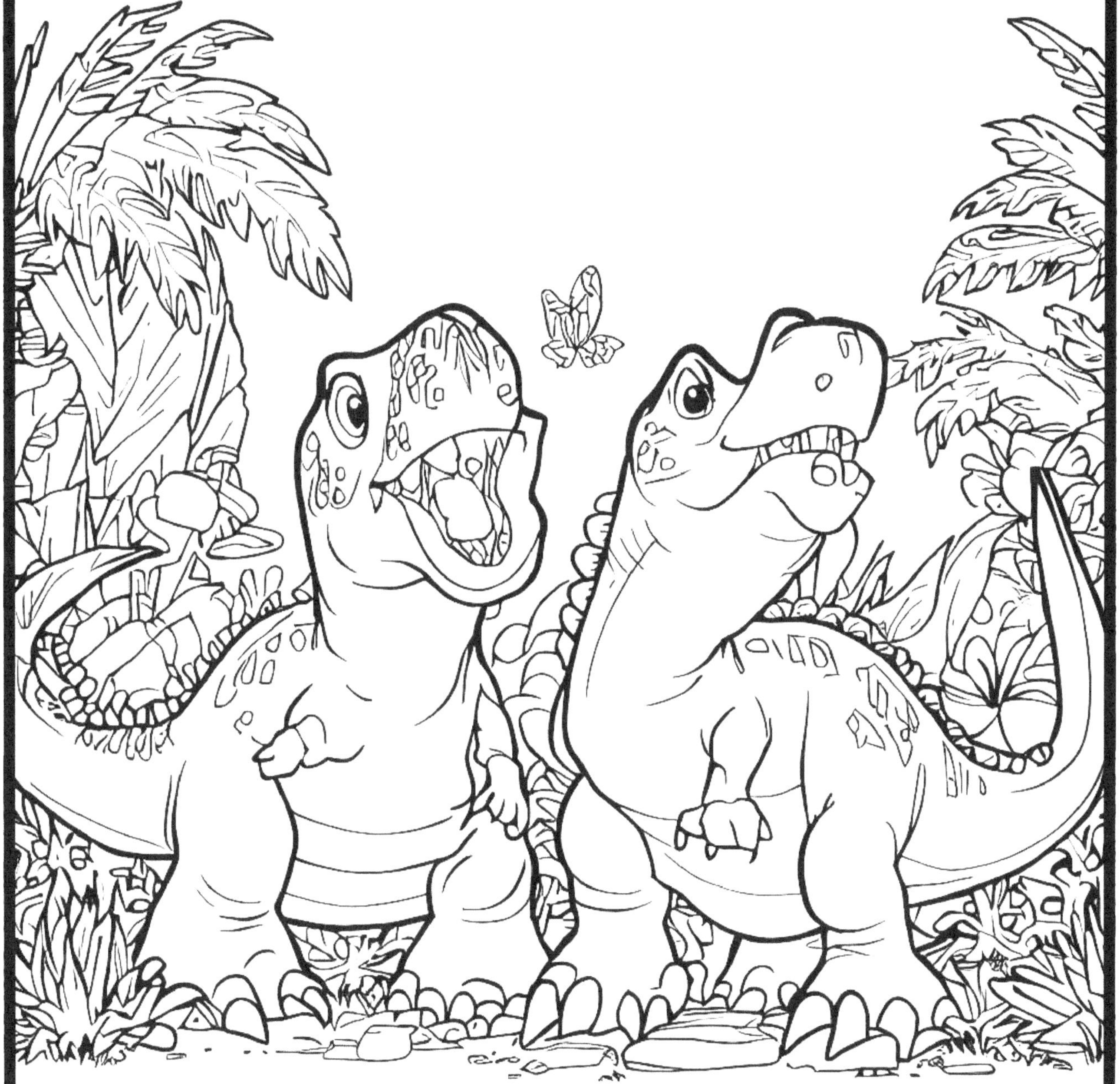

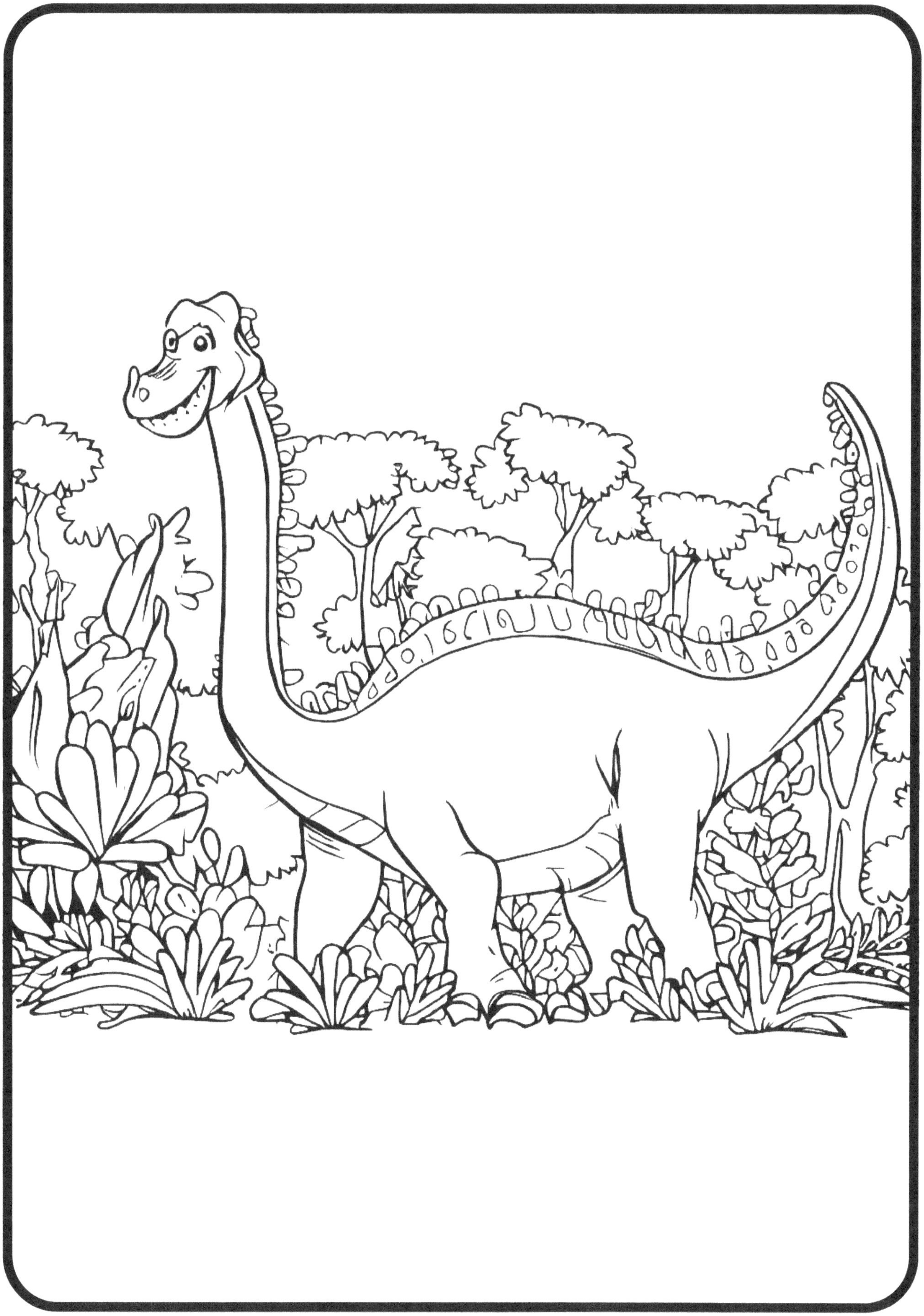

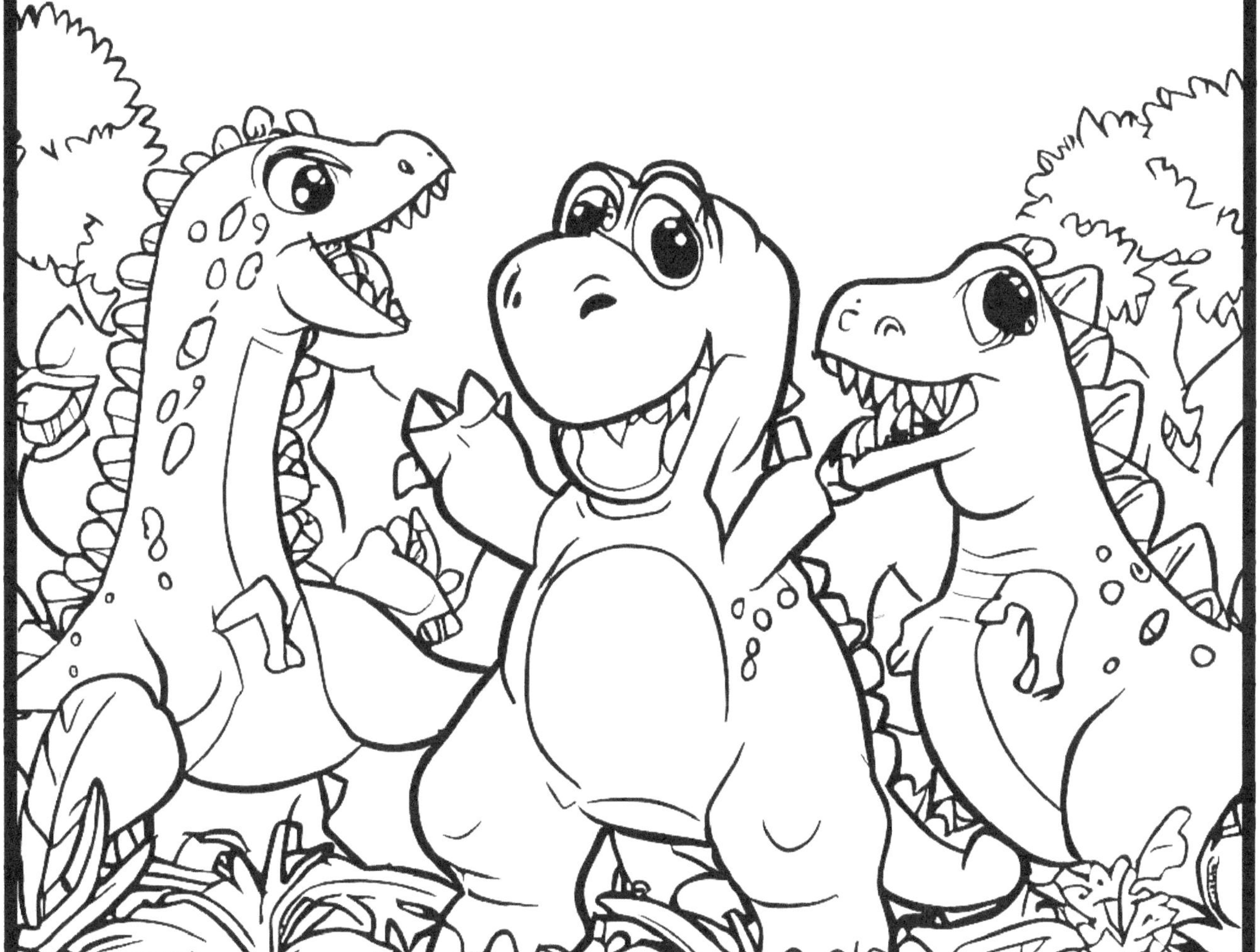

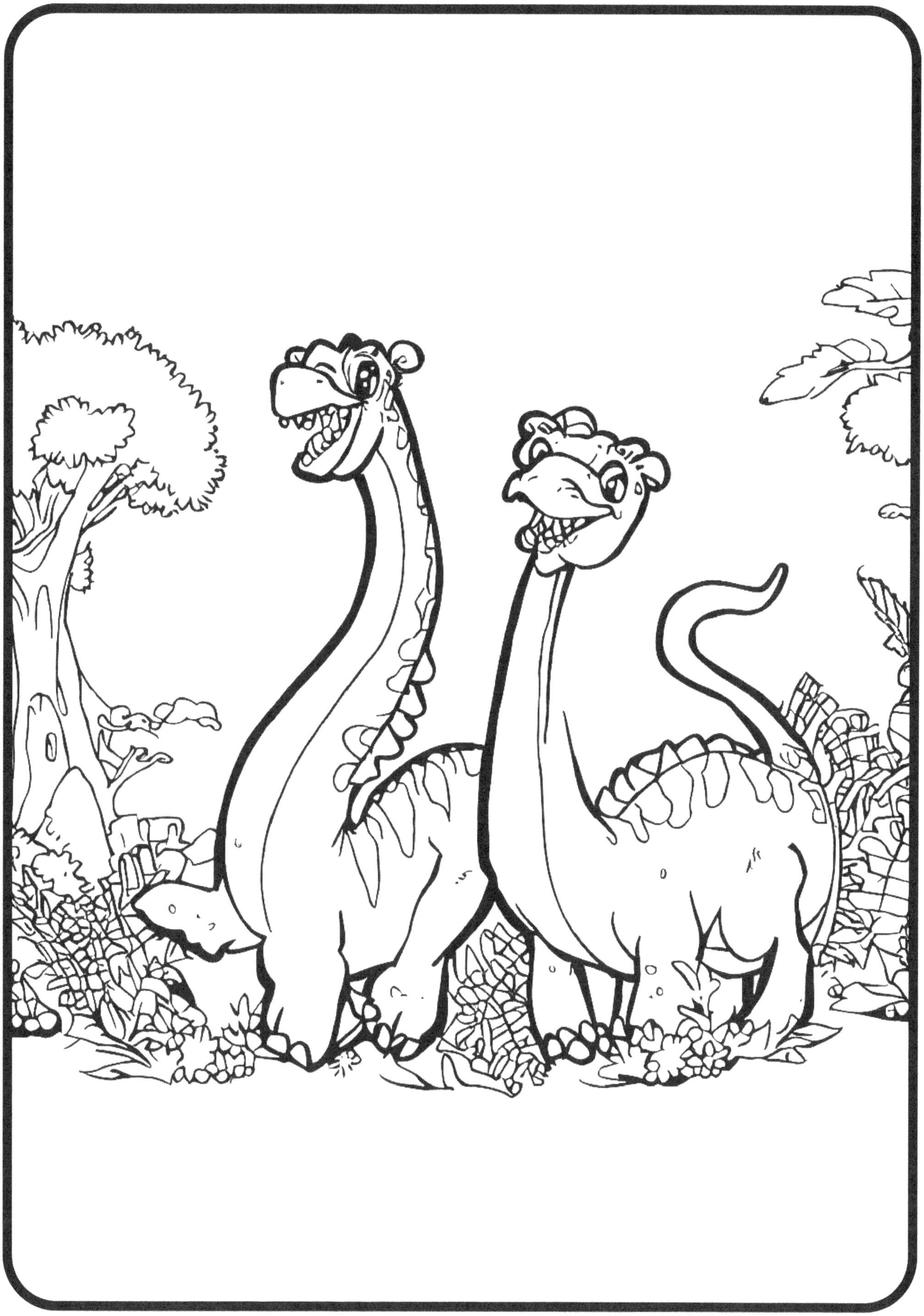

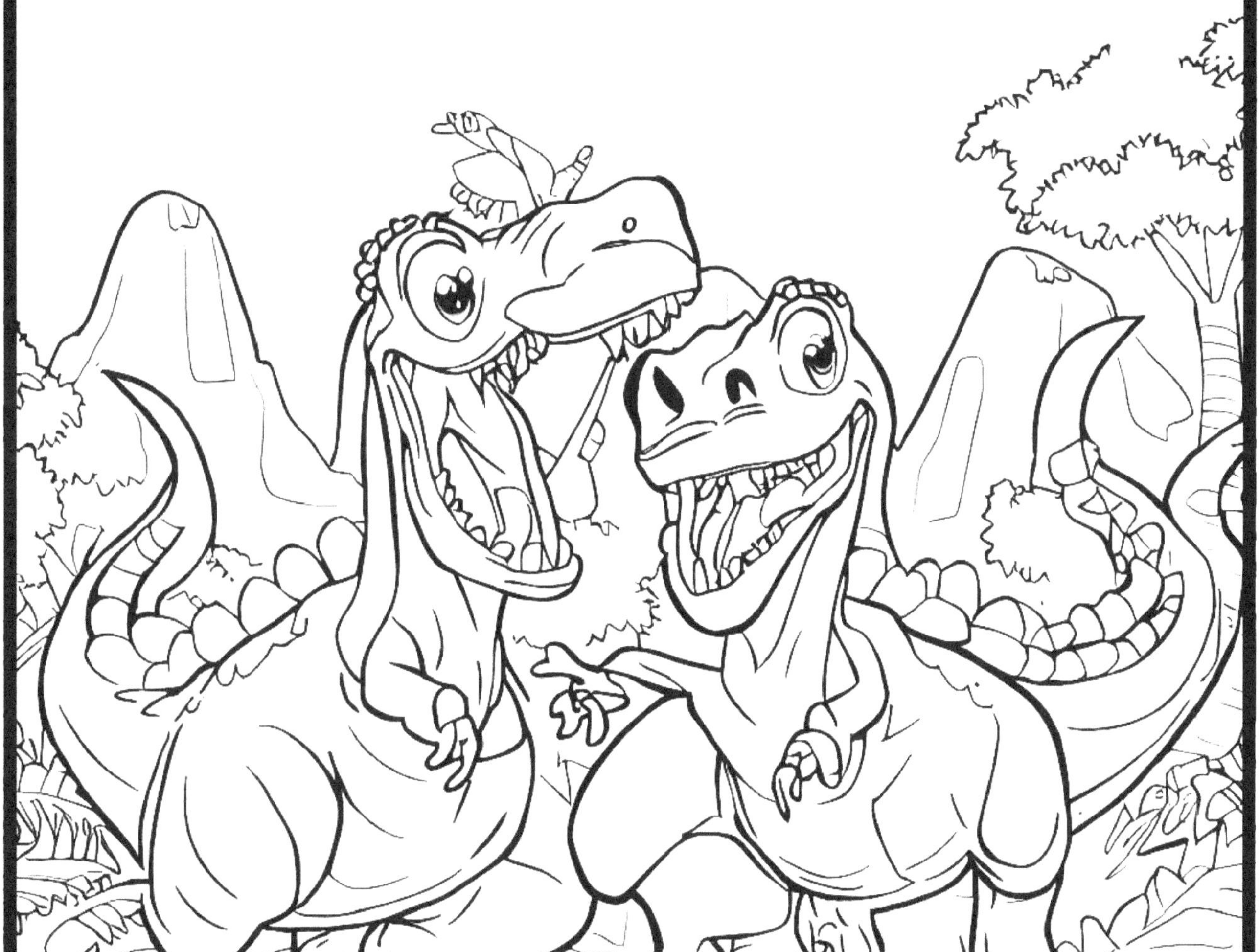

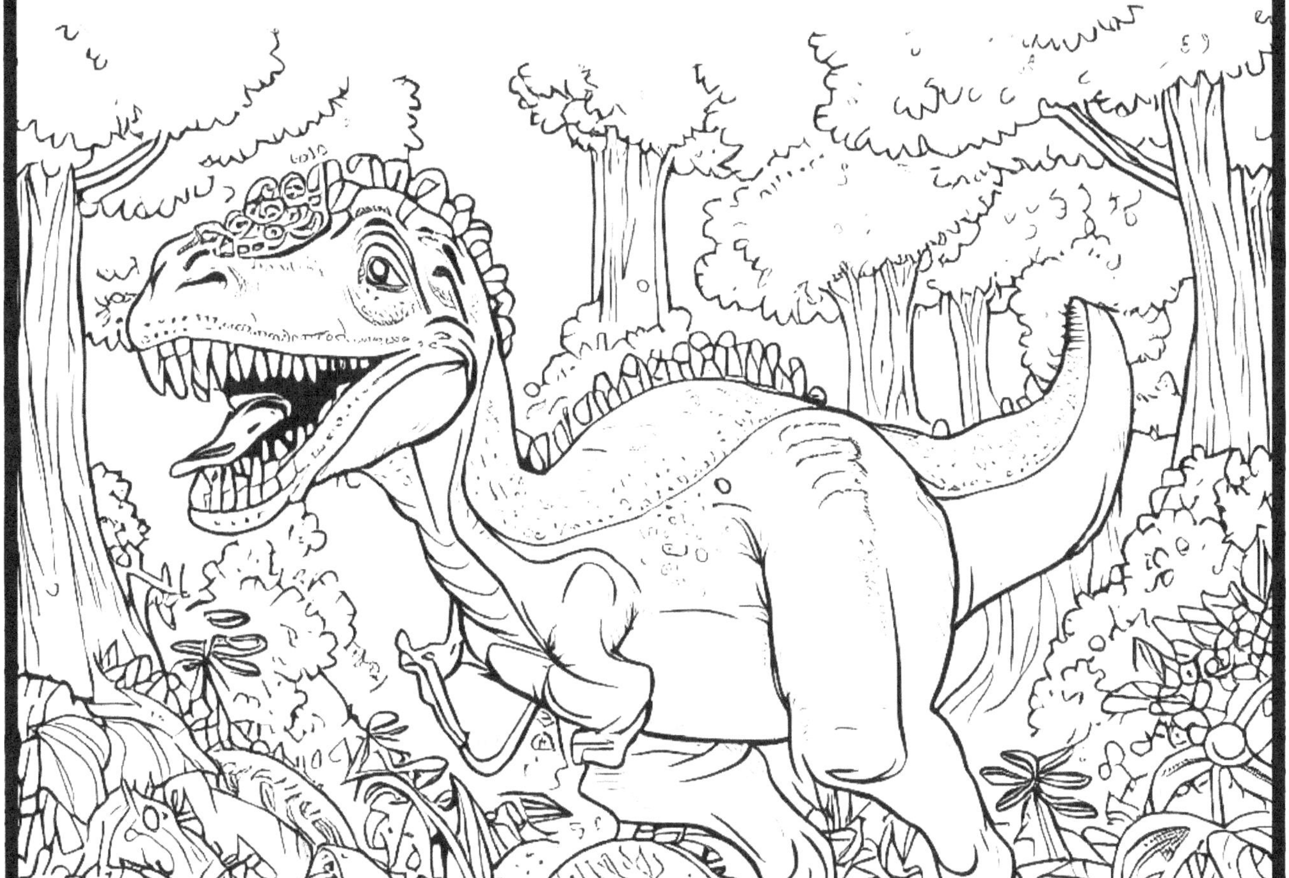

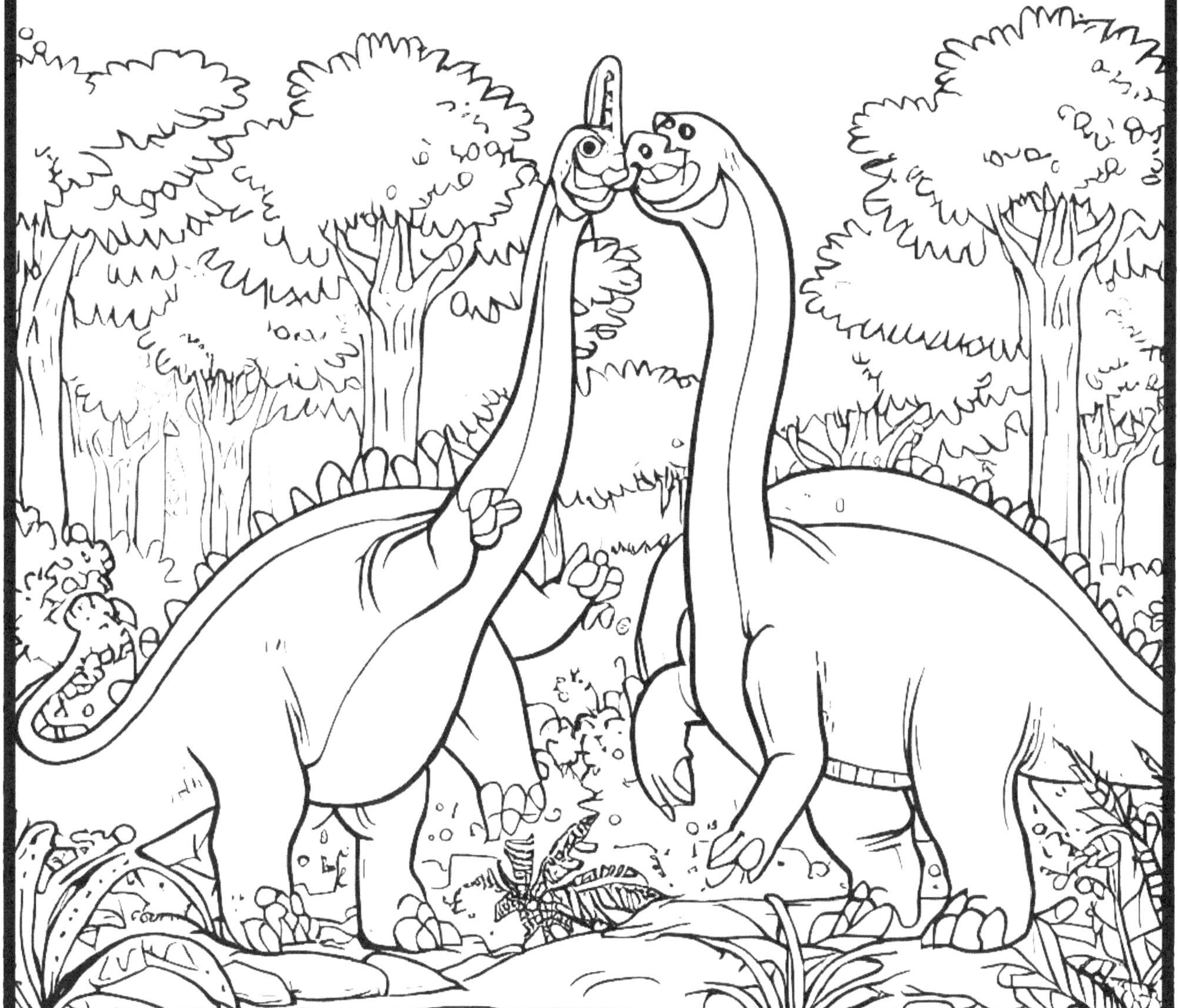

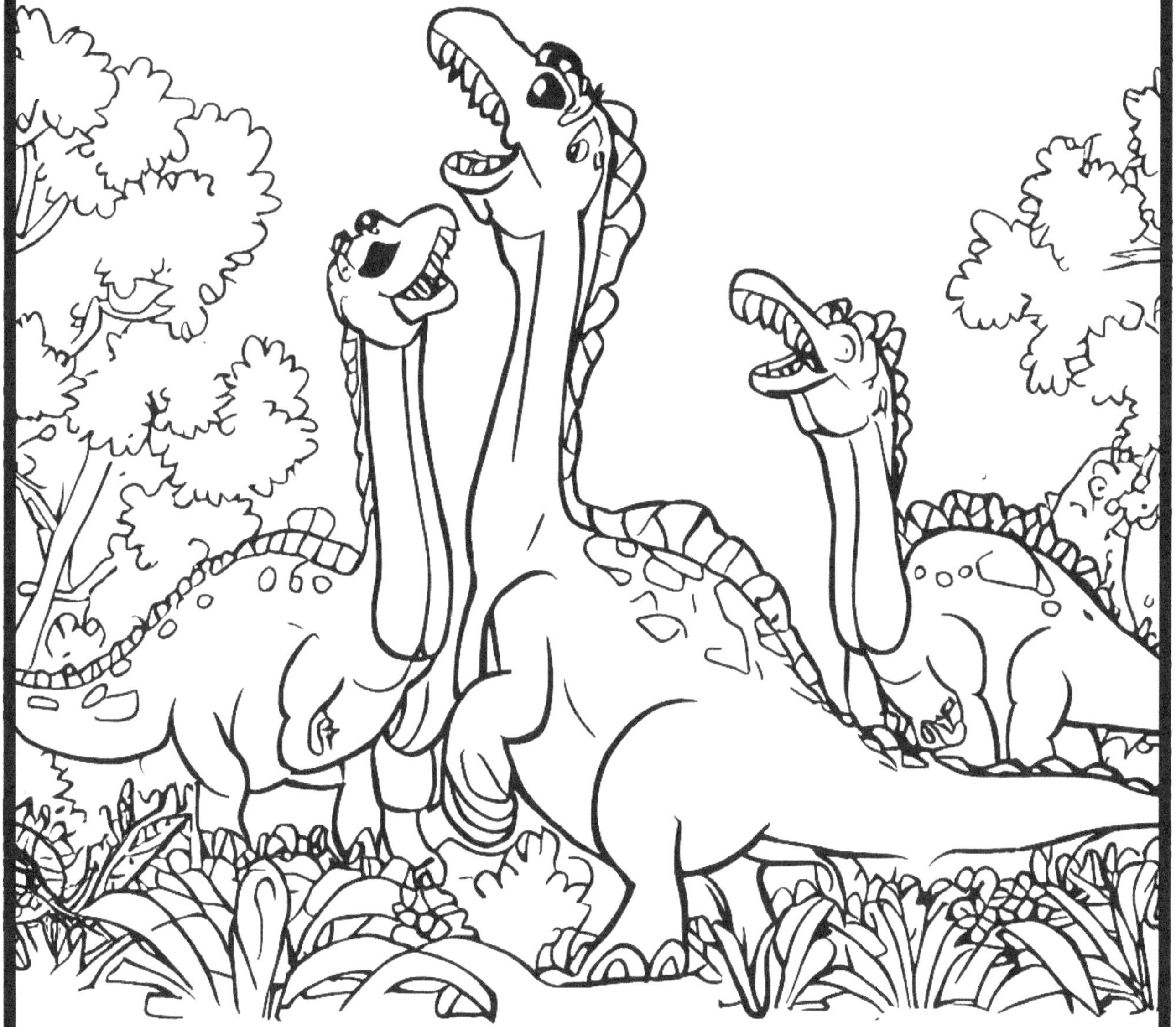

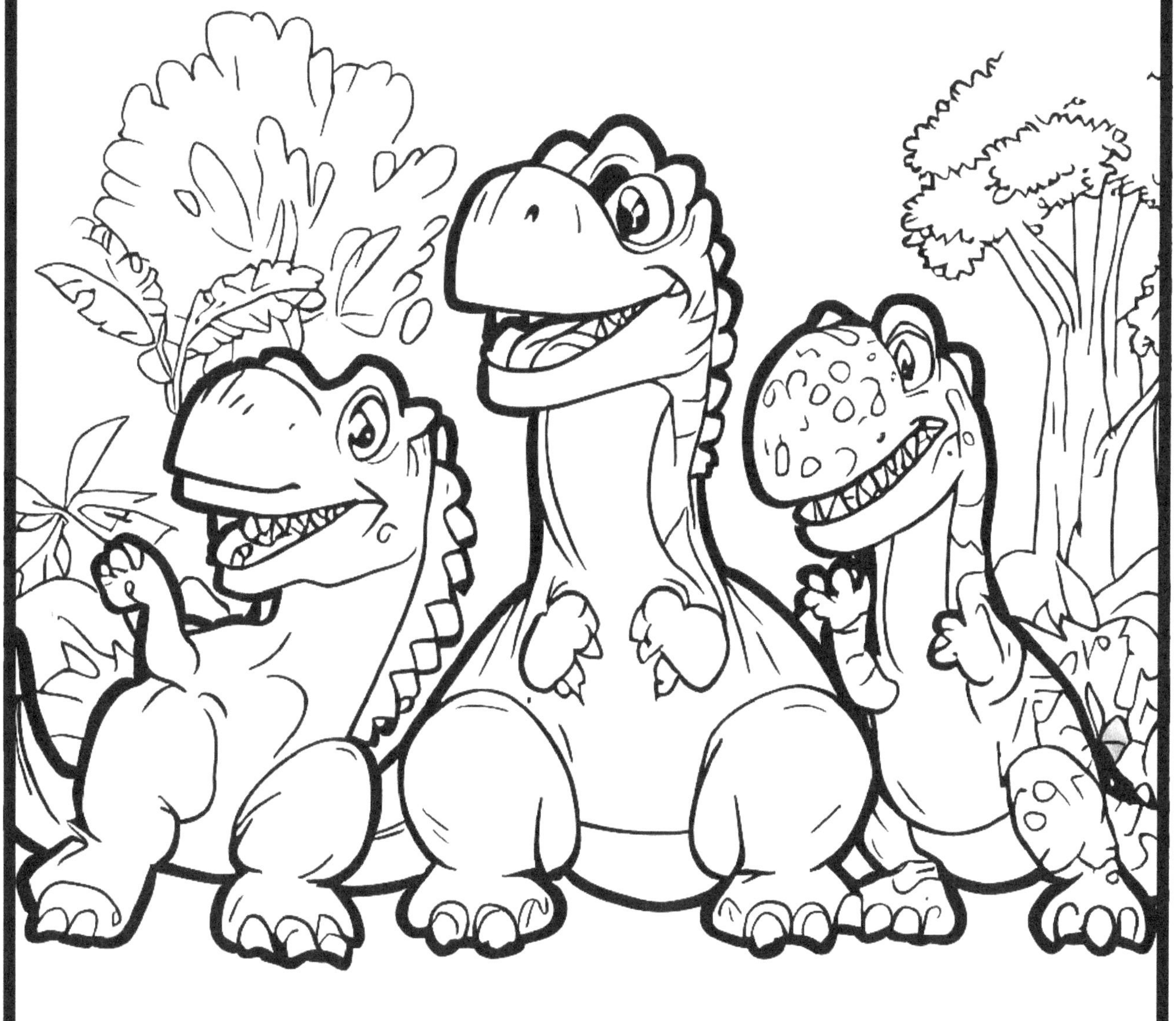

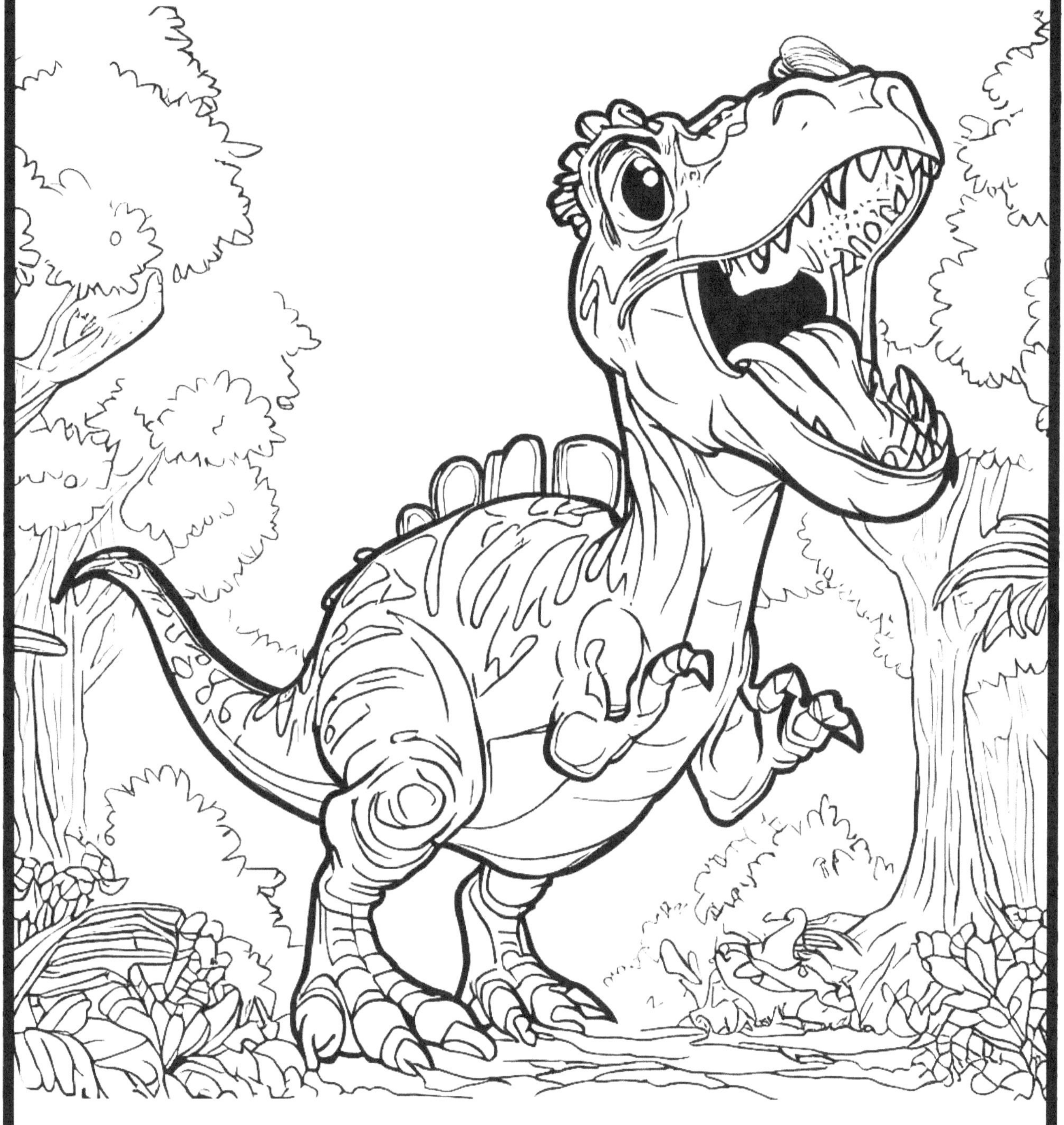

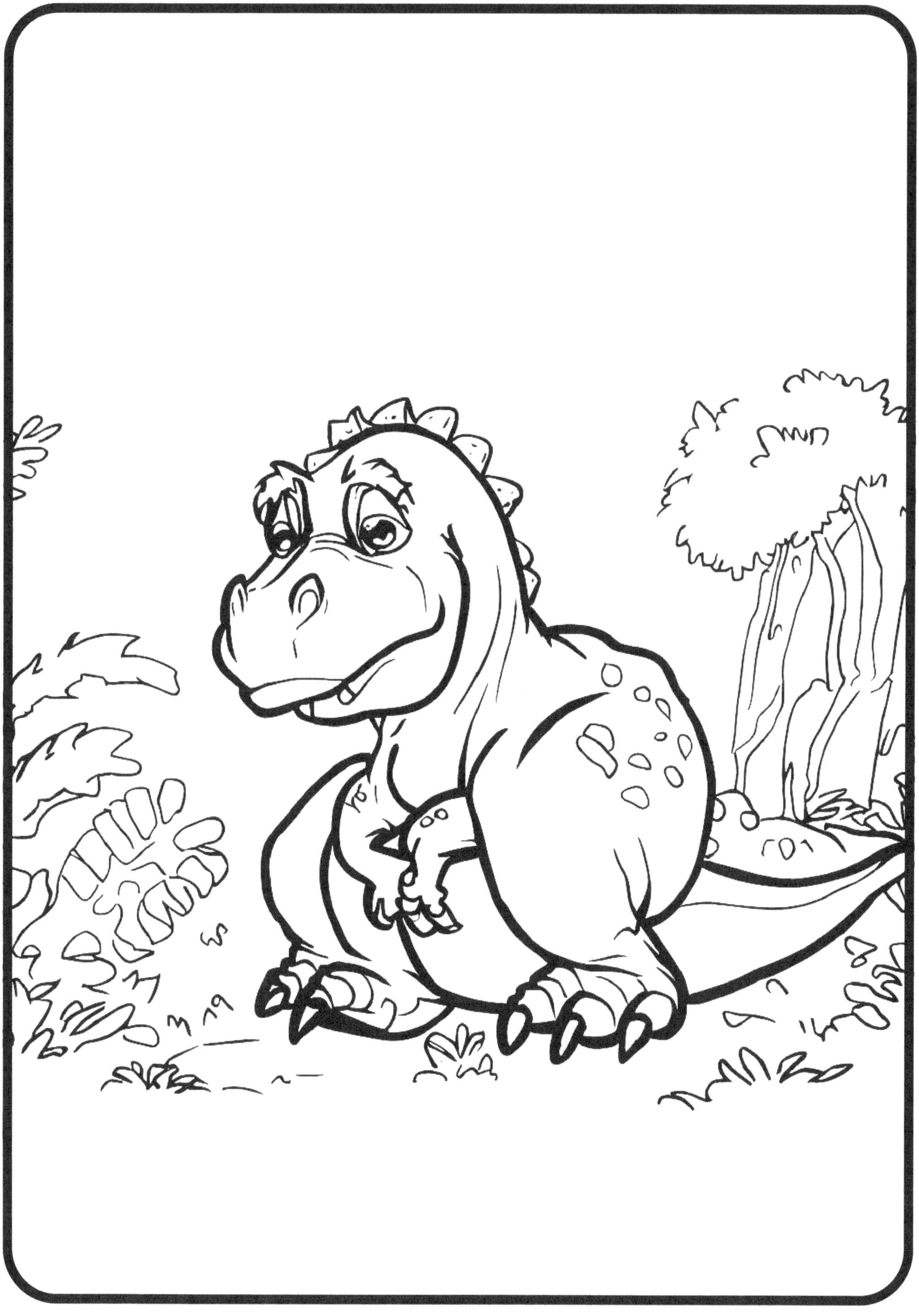

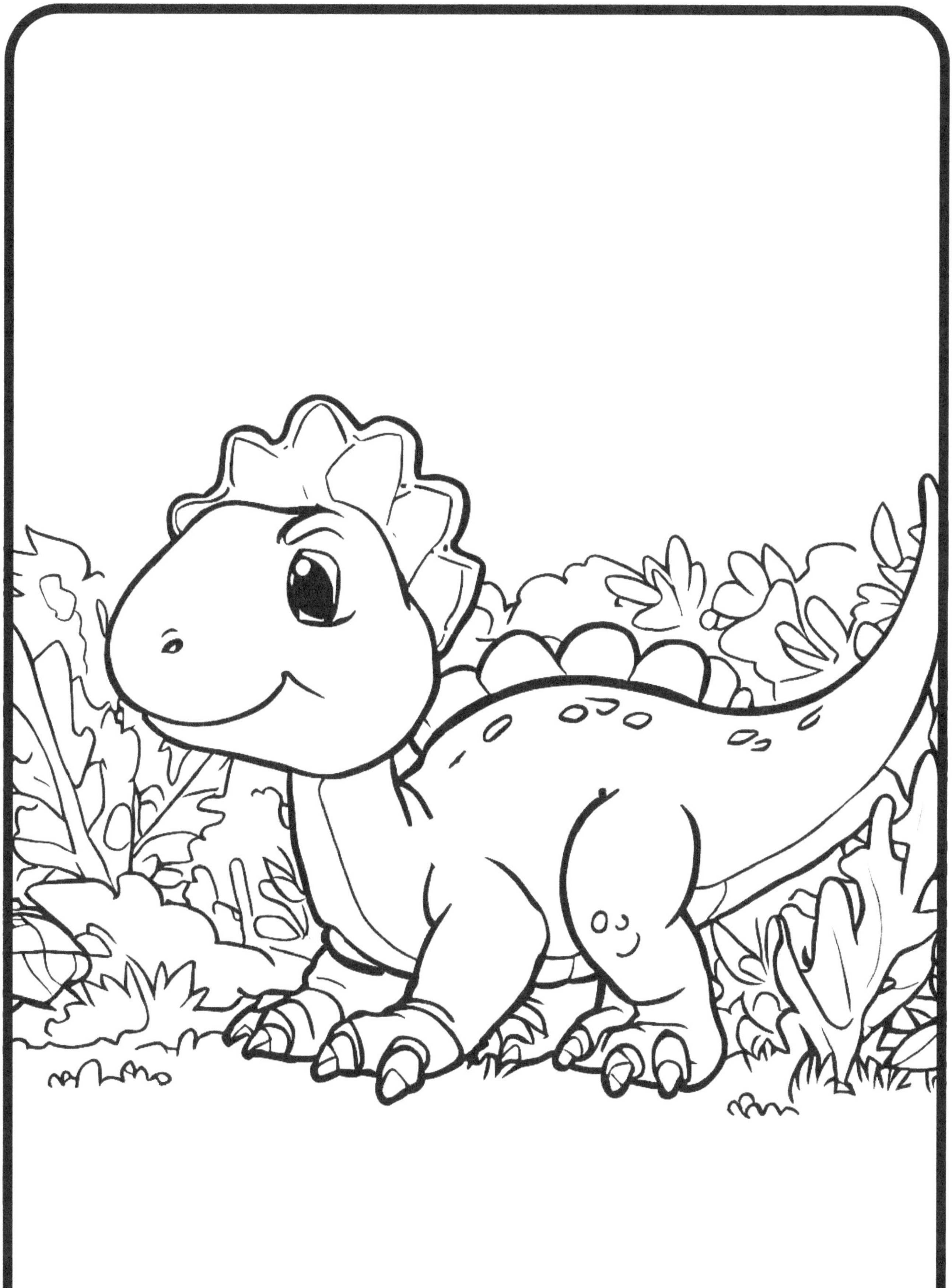

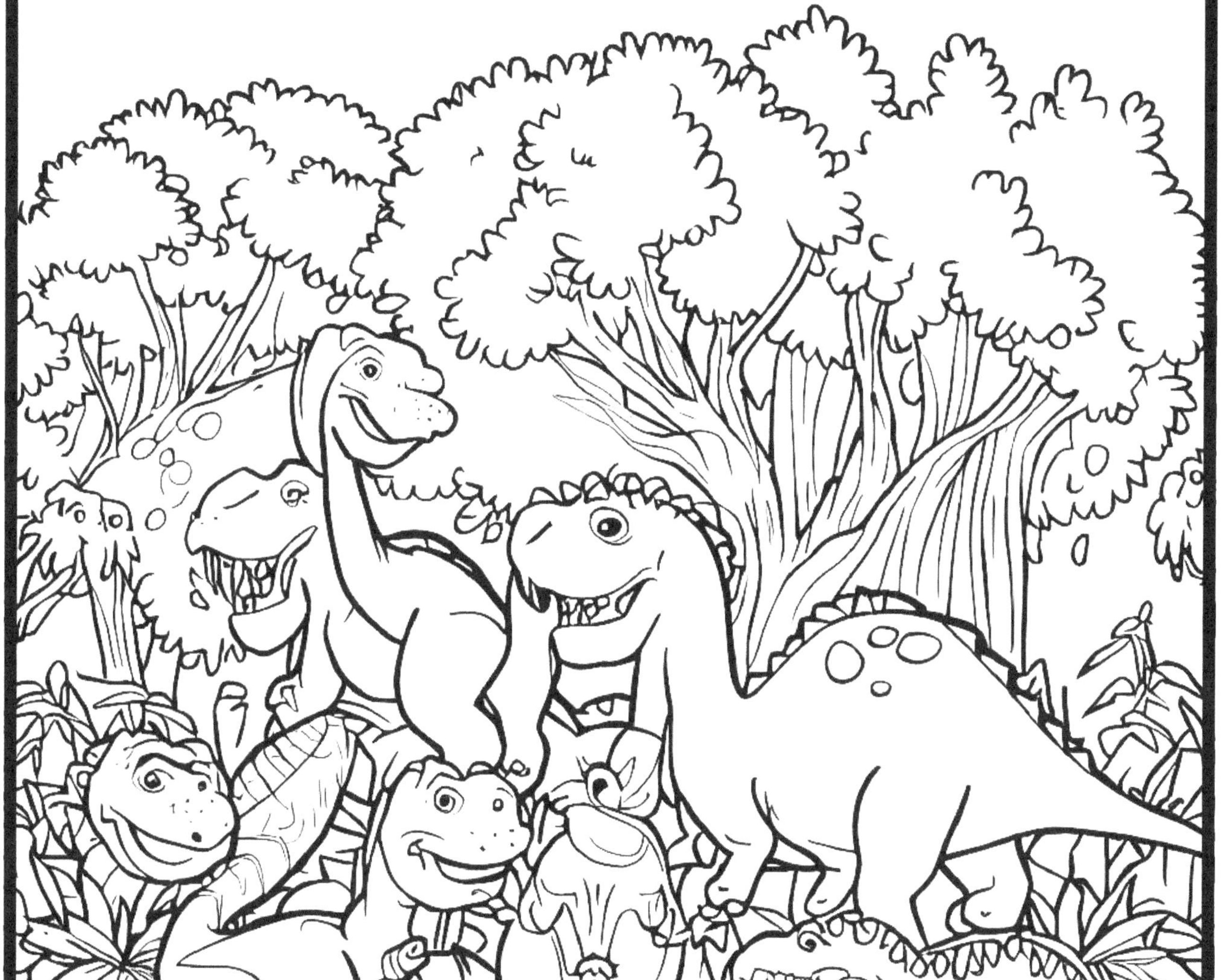

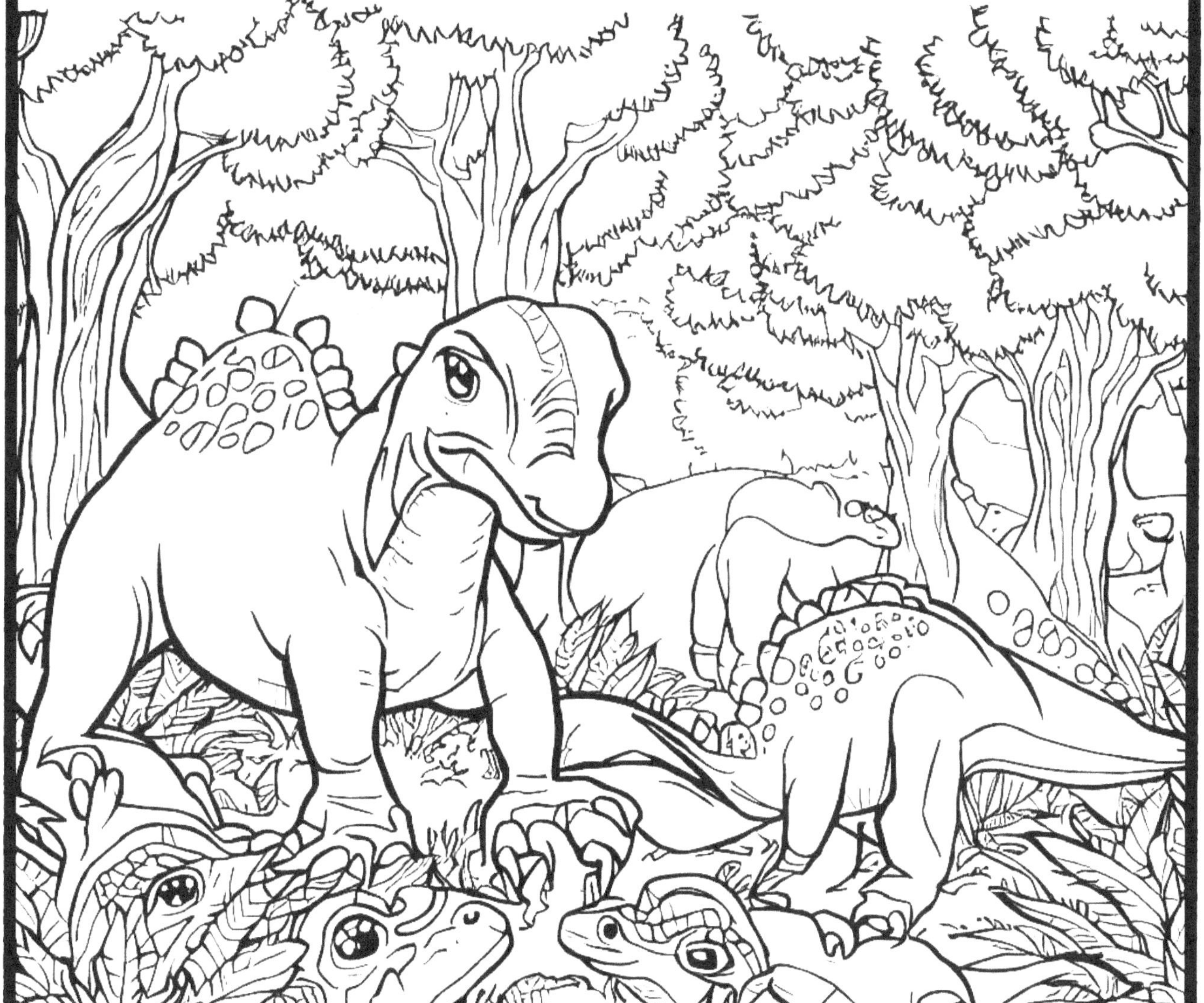

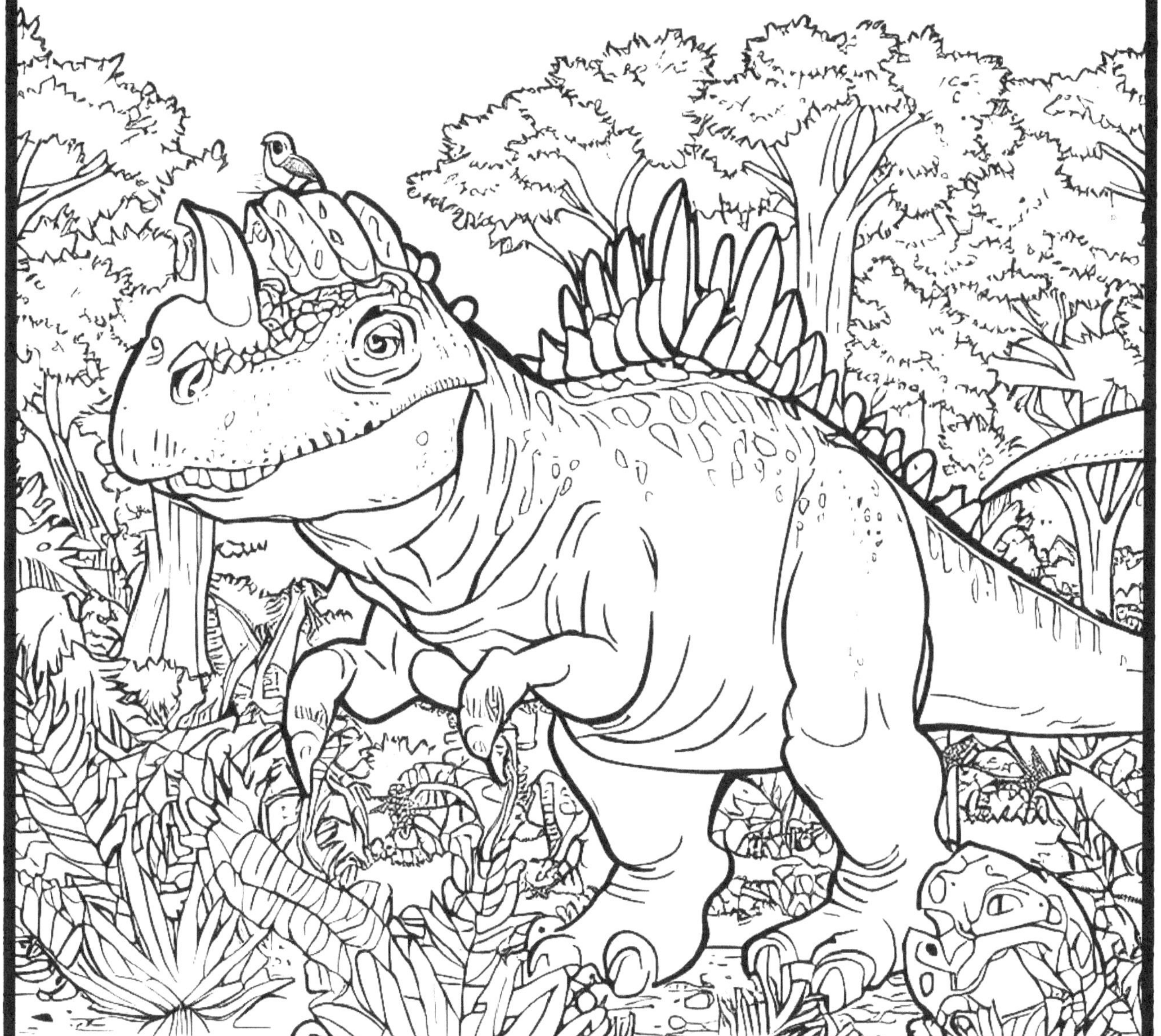

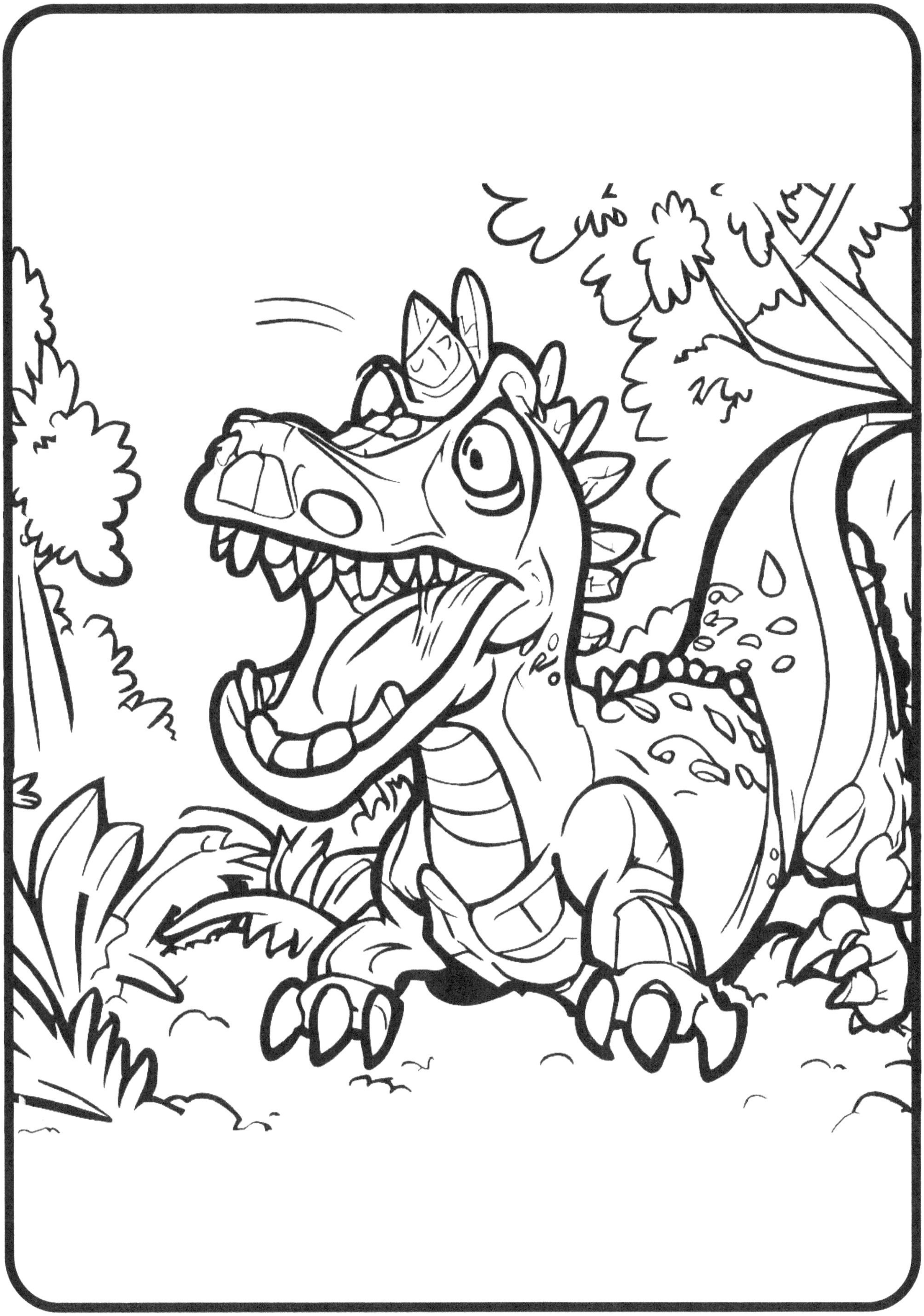

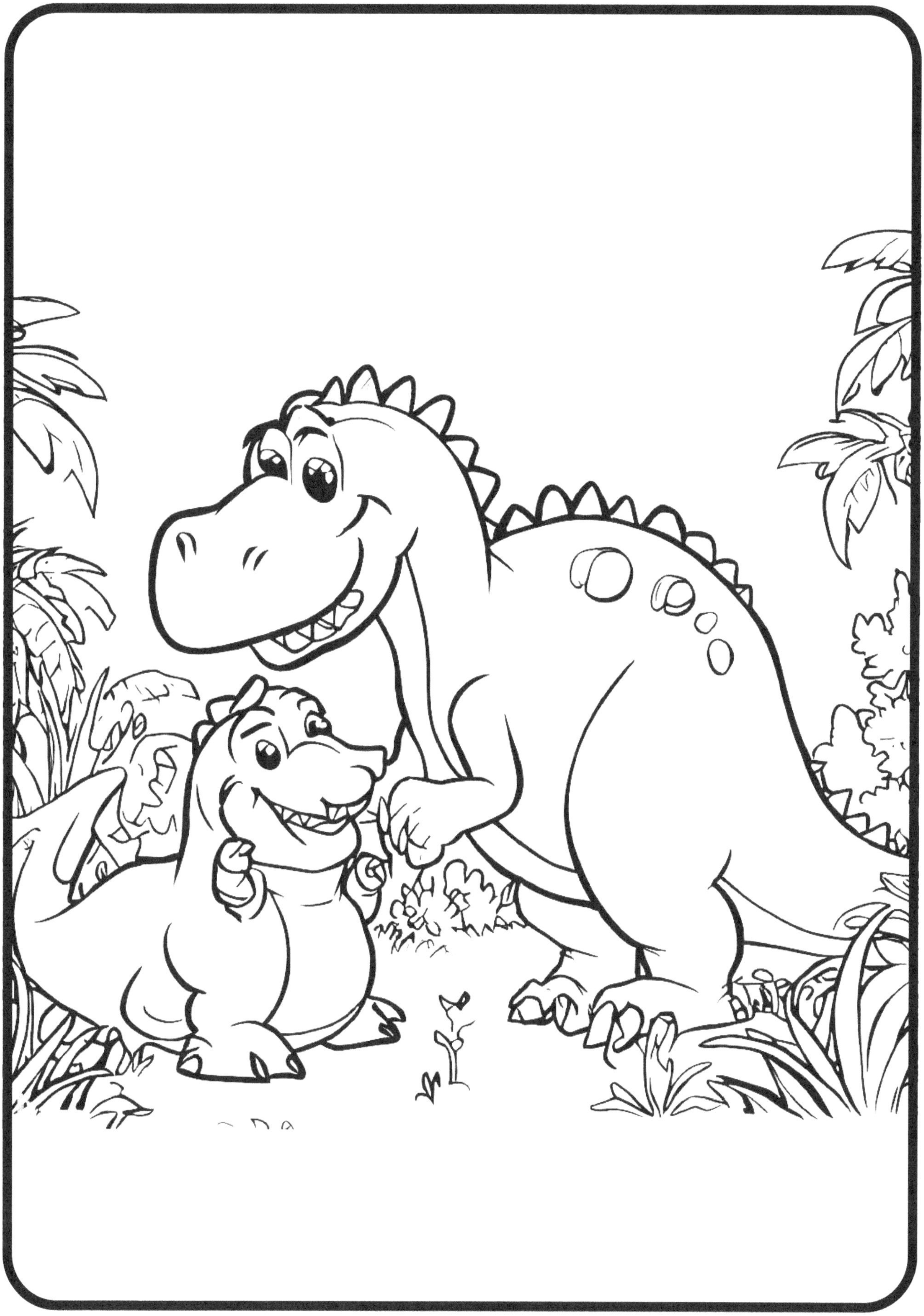

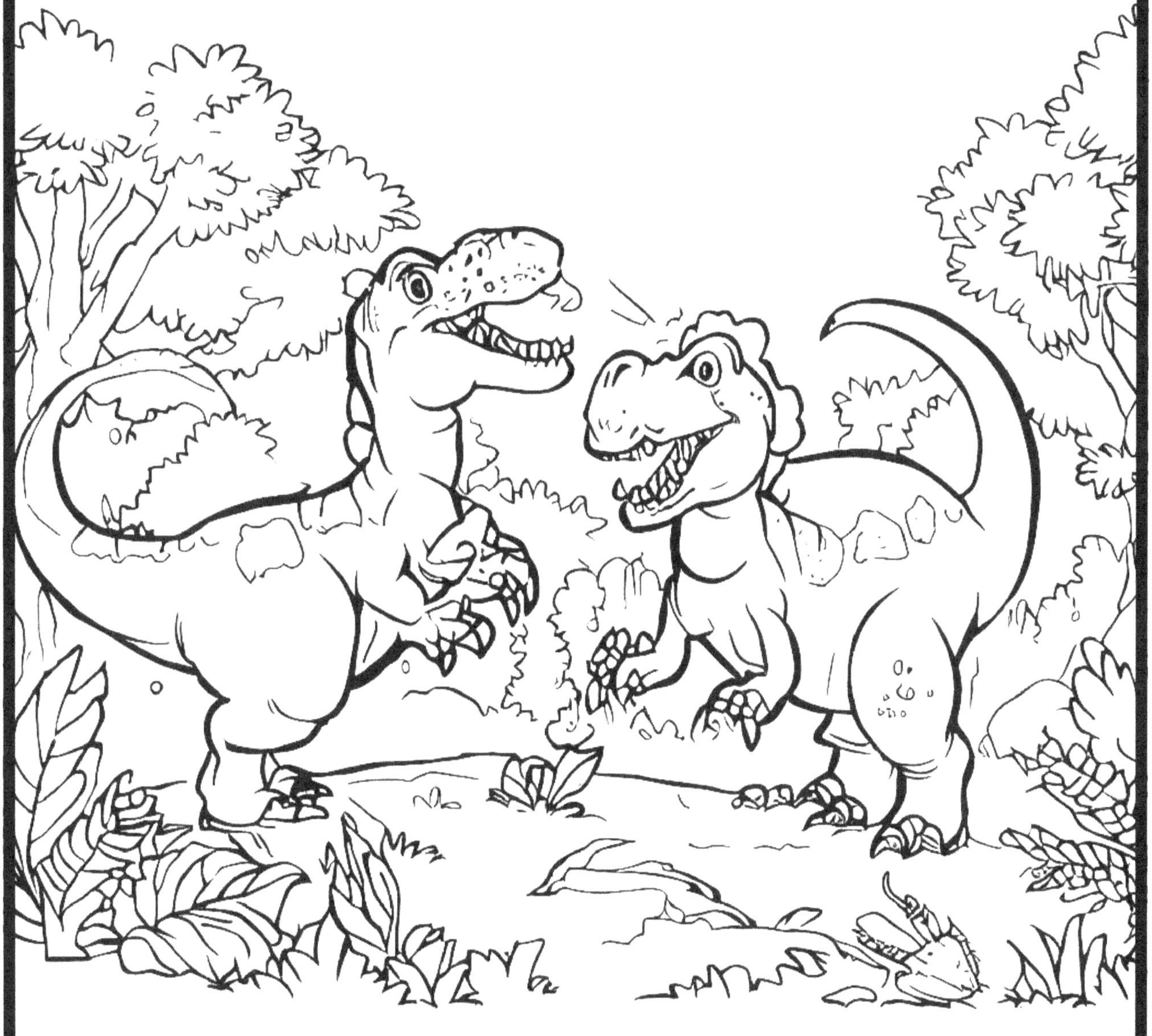

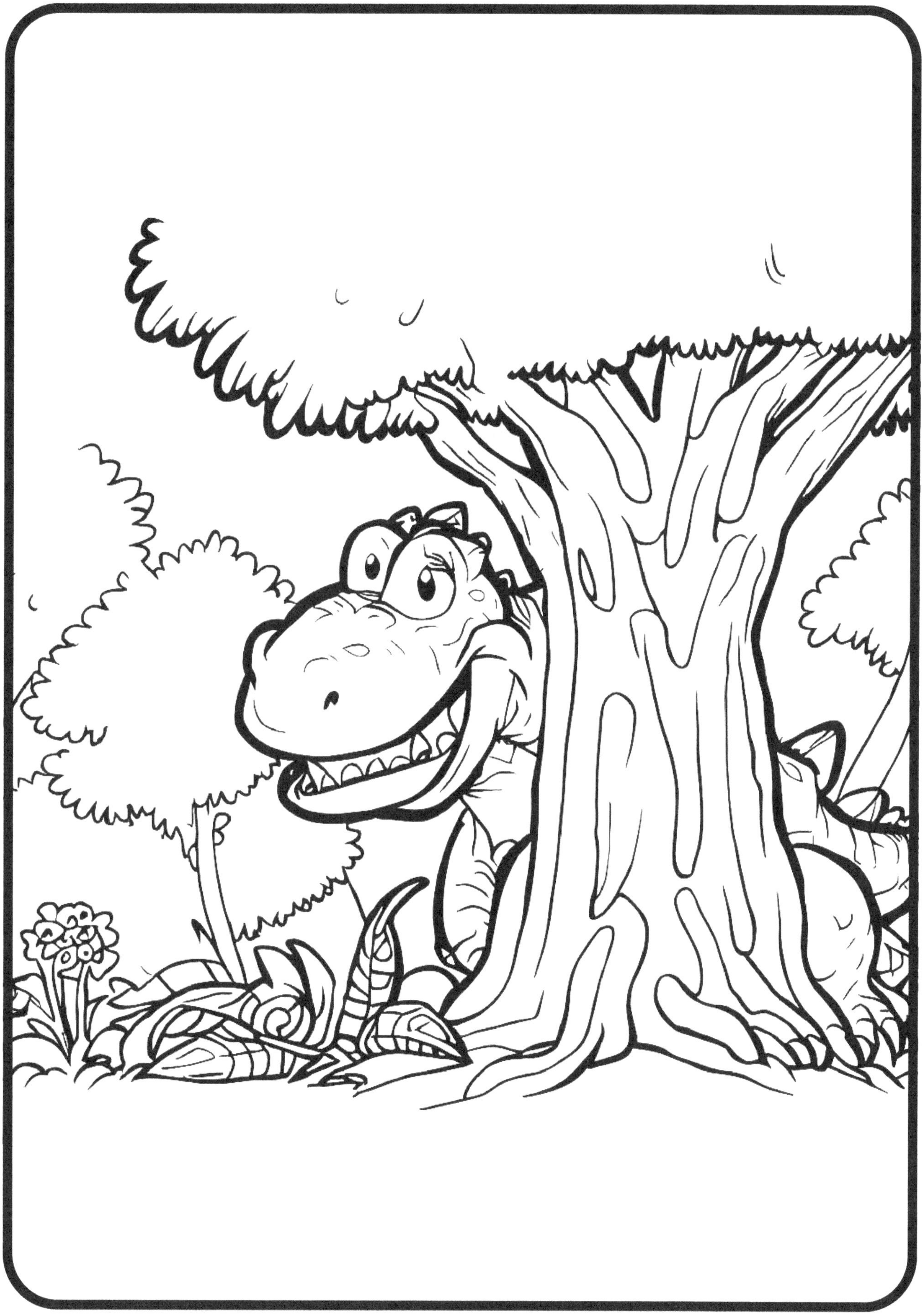

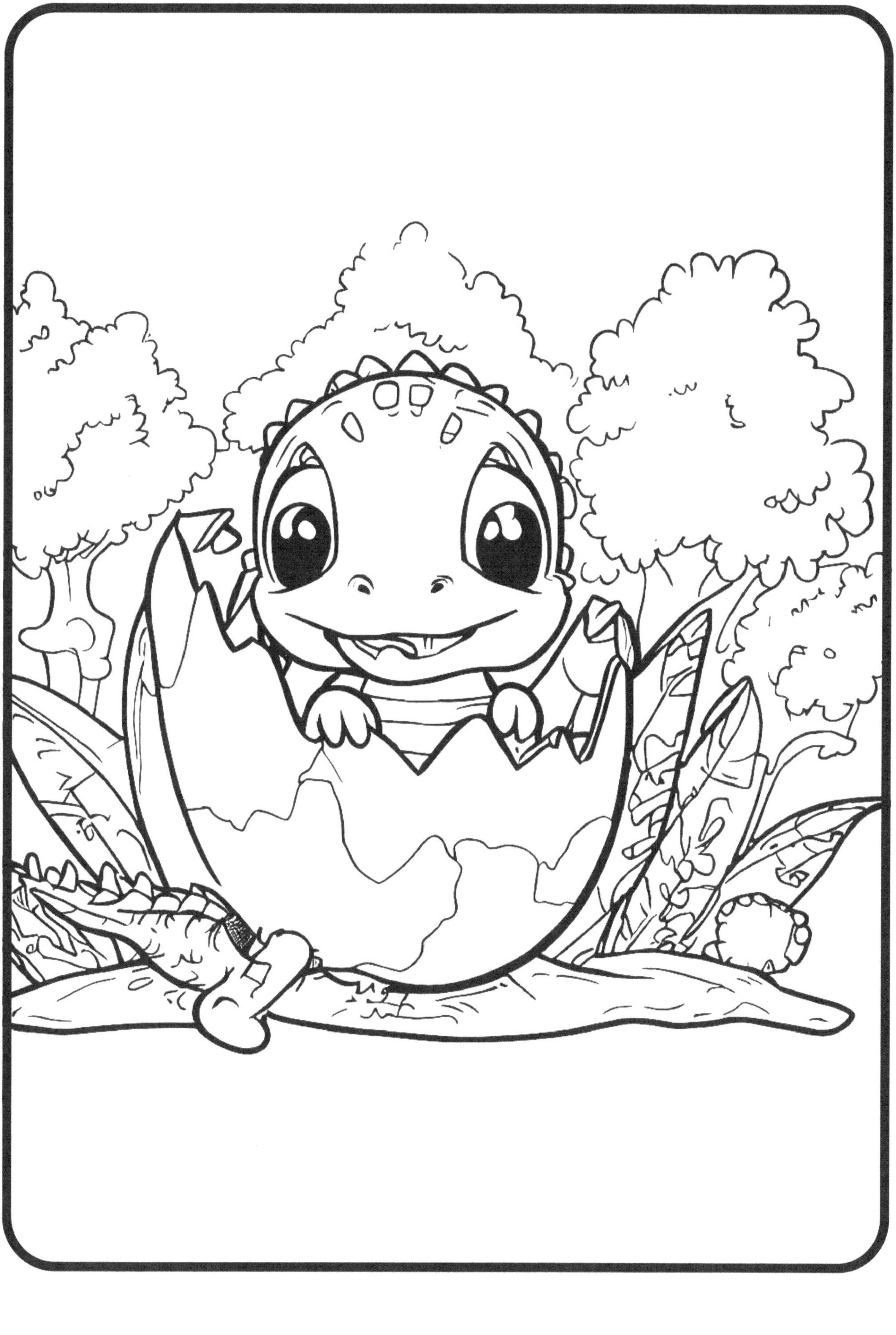

www.ingramcontent.com/pod-product-compliance
Lightning Source LLC
Chambersburg PA
CBHW081457220526
45466CB00008B/2684
* 9 7 9 8 3 9 7 6 6 7 2 7 2 *